Raised
a
Warrior

Raised
a
Warrior

A Memoir of Soccer,
Grit, and Leveling the
Playing Field

Susie Petruccelli

APOLLO
PUBLISHERS

CONTENTS

Gratefully dedicated to girls around the world and the teams that help me through life, especially the Harvard Women's Soccer Team.

*For Madi, Luca, Marco and Armando.
And Foudy, for telling me to "Get 'er done!"*

In loving memory of Meg Berté Owen, Liz McNamee, Leslie Poole, Katie Urbanic Moore, Molly Lynch, Cori Rising, Aaron Villegas, Matt Stauffer and Vikki Orvice. The goals are up, the music blasting, the everlasting joy of the game in our hearts.

*Special thanks to my brother Tom DeLellis,
Kely Nascimento-DeLuca and Ian Ridley.*

And for all of you out there who were chanting, "Equal pay."

It was like a slow-rising sun, gradually dawning on me—part of an awakening shared and accelerated by others, all of us coming to the same understanding and building momentum for change in the world.

    —*Melinda Gates,* The Moment of Lift

No person in the United States shall, on the basis of sex, be excluded from participation in, be denied the benefits of, or be subjected to discrimination under any education program or activity receiving Federal financial assistance.

    —*Title IX of the United States Education Amendments of 1972*

INTRODUCTION

As I sat down to write this book, I saw an opportunity like a seam that opens up on the field between two defenders during a match. And I knew that my teammates would see it too and do everything they could to get in behind. Through the process of researching and writing the early versions of this book—meant to be a tribute to my Harvard soccer teammates and everything we shared on and off the field—I started to see that I might have found a way to make a difference. And that's when my life took an unexpected turn.

Growing up as a soccer player in a non-soccer-loving country, I always felt like I had work to do. It became a competition in my young mind: me vs. the (as yet) non-soccer-loving world. I wanted soccer to have a fair share of television time along with baseball and American football, which dominated the channels in houses in my neighborhood. I wanted soccer players to be adored by America too, like the Joe Montanas and Babe Ruths of American sports lore. I wanted to sit at a dinner table where everyone was arguing passionately about soccer. I didn't know yet that there were other countries in the world where that was happening, where soccer was king. When I found this out, I thought I had been born in the wrong country.

When soccer finally started to appear on American television, it didn't come with an equal amount of girls' soccer, which was disappointing. But I had faith in soccer people. In my world, soccer was the equal sport. Much later I learned that I was lucky to have been born

1

in my soccer-ignoring country at a time when girls' soccer had begun an astonishing wave of growth.

My love for the game kept growing but I had a lot to learn. I lived a sheltered childhood and the news frightened me so I tuned it out. I grew up not learning about current events around the world. I grew up believing that wars had finite endings with a winner and a loser. Our history books say we won World War II but lost Vietnam. I thought we had won the civil rights movement and the women's rights movement. I didn't know there was further to go.

By the time I was in high school, my club soccer team was winning important tournaments. My high school team won our division's Southern California championship (California was so big it was divided in two). I had trophies and medals, including a couple of special ones for Most Valuable Player. I had the great honor of playing with and against women who played on the US youth and women's national teams. I was recruited to play soccer by some of the best universities in America. And yet, I had absolutely no clue how or by whom that path had been created or how rare and valuable those opportunities were, and I didn't show anywhere near the character of a true champion until the moment I said goodbye to the game I loved.

I had been raised to be a warrior by my father. He taught me to show no mercy on or off the sports field. But being my own kind of warrior—a spiritual warrior, a champion on and off the field, a student of the world in search of a way to give back to it—was something I was barely beginning to see through the fog.

PROLOGUE

Before the neighbor put up a chain-link fence and the climbing vines turned it into a leafy green wall, the window of the back bedroom of my parents' house had looked out beyond the little soccer field that was our backyard and across to the tall buildings of downtown Los Angeles in the distance. I had shared that back bedroom with my identical twin sister. We'd moved in when we were two years old, two matching blonde toddlers. But there were depths to us that were not the same, and before we were seven she had moved out, angry, in the middle of the night to another room as far away as she could get.

Now I was back in that bedroom after being away at college on the East Coast for two years. The bunkbeds were long gone, replaced by a king-sized bed with puffy, floral bedding for guests. The old me was long gone too.

I heard my dad's car pull into the driveway. His approach always had the same effect: a tightening of the chest. I heard his car door open and close, followed by the sound of the front door. I heard muffled voices as he spoke briefly to my mom in the kitchen and then he sat down as usual in his chair in front of the television with a beer. Some things hadn't changed.

I knew what I had to do. I took a deep breath, stood up and faced the mirrored closet door. The person looking back at me looked like a wreck. I saw a loser, a selfish fuck-up. I deserved whatever was coming my way. I pulled on the knitted hat that I held in my hand. I looked more normal with the hat on, but I wasn't normal. Just a few years ago I had felt strong, my whole life in front of me. Now so much adrenaline was pumping through my body I might as well have been looking out the open door of an airplane 12,000 feet in the air. Yet I was weak and permanently broken.

No one had seen me yet except the young woman who did it and my friend Romi, both of whom had tried valiantly to talk me out of it. I wasn't that surprised the young hair stylist had been afraid. I must have seemed crazy as I coaxed her into it.

"Don't worry," I'd said. "This is on me, I promise you. I won't hold you responsible. This is my decision."

I'd been surprised that Romi wasn't on board. She was like me, rebelling against the social confines around us, but she'd just grimaced and hugged her knees to her chest in one of the other stylist's chairs.

"No, Susie. Don't do it," she had pleaded. The reality was setting in and she was afraid.

Seeing her doubt my decision filled me with dread. I'd thought she would get it. I'd thought I had at least one person in my corner. Was she afraid that I would be too ugly? No, that wasn't like her. Her fear was probably of my dad. She didn't want my dad to know she'd had anything to do with it. I'd realized then that I would be on my own when I showed him.

But none of the thoughts racing through my head could have stopped me at that point. I'd made up my mind. I wasn't afraid of being ugly. I wasn't afraid of looking like a boy. I wasn't afraid of being different. I wasn't afraid at all. In fact, in that moment I'd felt calm. I needed a fresh start, a second chance to be a better person. I needed to hold down the power button and force a hard reset.

The tattoo had been extremely impulsive. I had gone by myself a day earlier. It was as if a higher power had guided me as a symbol came to my mind—a small oval with two concentric rings around it—and a strong force swept through me. *Hope.* I'd searched the house for paper and a pen, quickly drawing the image in black felt-tip marker on a yellow legal pad, then grabbed my car keys and driven myself to Old Town Pasadena where all the tattoo shops are. The little symbol was on the back of my right shoulder within two hours.

My life had imploded and putting it back together had started to feel like too much. All I knew was that the tattoo was some kind of marker of a rebirth. A permanent reminder of a rock bottom. I wasn't sure yet if it was breadcrumbs to follow or avoid.

But the tattoo hadn't been the end of it, and the next day my hair had had to go. Maybe subconsciously I knew that rebuilding myself from nothing was going to be like growing hair: you can't see it happening day by day but if you have patience and faith, growth happens. Whatever had made me do it, I'd found the very beginnings of healing when I gave myself that time—the time it takes to grow your hair back.

But I knew none of this would make sense to my dad. I had been raised to be tough and to show no fear, so that's what I did. I walked down the hallway, around the back of his well-worn chair and stood between him and the television. I felt tall looking down at him. I felt exposed. I waited until he looked up from his work, his beer within arm's reach on the side table. The fear in my gut was intense and I knew I'd have to keep the tattoo hidden for now.

I put a big smile on my face. My mom walked over from the kitchen sink to see what I was up to. Her presence next to him made him look up. Meeting his gaze, I whipped the hat off my head and said: "Ta da!"

PART 1
LA TIMES

My father once got into a fistfight with an opposing coach at my brother's baseball game while I was watching from the bleachers. Another time, he dragged a man laying tiles in our house into the street and punched him while we watched from the backyard. There was a scary chaos that came with both of those confrontational, unpredictable moments that made the ground feel unsteady under my feet. But what I took away was that sometimes an injustice calls for a fight, and that you don't back down even if it means breaking rules about appropriate behavior. I felt like he would also have my back if I ever needed it, just like he'd had my brother's, so I had his back and I never stopped wanting to be just like him. Maybe that's why it hurt so much when he said I couldn't play his sport. He was most proud when we ignored pain, so I ignored this pain too. But being denied the chance to show him how good I could be at his game because I was a girl hurt. Like when you fall off your bike and slide along the ground with nothing between your skin and the street, it burned.

On Saturdays, when I was a kid growing up in South Pasadena, California, my dad would take my twin sister and me to the local junior high while he ran around the field and dropkicked a football into the air over and over again. As it rose and fell, he would sprint as fast as he could to make the catch. Without even meaning to, perhaps—for all I know, he was just getting us out of the house so my mother could enjoy some time without her four young children underfoot—he was teaching us that, in order to be good at something, you had to practice it. A lot. But at the time, I thought we were playing. I loved the way the muscles looked in his legs. The ball, which felt as heavy as a watermelon when I picked it up, sounded like a rocket leaving his laces. I ran around trying to copy his every move, worried I was going to accidentally get in his way and have him come crashing down on top of me.

A former full-back for the Stanford University football team whose father was a former Loyola University quarterback, my dad taught us all to love sports as much as he did. Before his freshman year in 1962, the *Los Angeles Times* mentioned him as "Tony DeLellis, the son of former Loyola star and coach by the same name." My mom was an avid fan as well. In fact, although I totally failed to appreciate her fandom and athleticism at the time ("Remember, I was the best bowler in my class at Stanford," she often interjected when we gave our father credit for our physical talents), she may have been the biggest sports fan of us all. She used to scream at the Stanford coach from the sidelines of home games when she was a student: "Put DeLellis in!" She hadn't even met my father yet; she just thought he was being underutilized.

In our home, in a hilly neighborhood just east of East Los Angeles, sports were the salve for our often-tense family dynamics. My older brothers, Tony and Tom, fought a lot. Katie and I—although identical twins—were as different on the inside as any two people could be. And my father, born during World War II, had a Depression-era mentality. His default state was grumpy; his default answers were variations on the word "no": absolutely not, don't even think about it, find something cheaper. My mom did her best to please him, happy to sideline her own career passions in that effort, but it wasn't easy. And I get it now, of course. Neither of my parents came from money. They were starting from scratch, young parents with more kids than they expected and big responsibilities.

My mom's father, a gambler and an alcoholic, left their family when my mom and her two brothers were young; her mother supported them by working nights as a nurse. My father's mother was a teacher. His father taught too, for a time. And coached and sold sporting goods and ran a small restaurant before eventually being persuaded to start a box distribution business to serve his friends, the Italian farmers who sold their produce in the market downtown. They needed someone they could trust in the box business, they said.

Before joining his father in the box business (at first just to fill in while my grandfather had cataract surgery), my dad tried a few engineering jobs and even a sweater manufacturing business. When he came home, he was exhausted and stressed. A hush would fall over the house when we heard his car pull into the driveway as we tried to stay out of trouble by cleaning up, doing homework, setting the table or practicing in the backyard. If a light was on in an empty room, he would grumble about the electricity. If there was a mess, we would hear about it. He once lined the four of us up on the driveway about a straw wrapper. He hated things he considered a waste of time or money, like anything with a brand name, or makeup for instance. The only time I ever saw my mom put on eye shadow before a night out, he said: "I don't know why you put that on, Marion. You look better without it."

It could have been a compliment if said in a nice tone, but the days were tough on my dad and things often came out of his mouth like he was frustrated with the world. She liked to dress up—she was proud of her looks—so if she wanted to have some fun with makeup sometimes, I didn't understand why that was so bad. Part of me wished she would respond to him. Say something back. But the other part of me understood why she thought better of it and went to take her makeup off. Sometimes it's not worth a fight.

Sports were something we could all agree on; they were the common bond that united us, a source of family pride dating back generations. My dad had played for the 1963 Stanford team that defeated Notre Dame for the first time. Papa, his father, was respected for his accomplishments as a quarterback at high school and then college. The *Los Angeles Times* had called him "the best football player, pound for pound, in these parts." Everyone knew him, or at least it seemed that way. When I was in high school, once in a while one of the boys from Loyola would ask me if I was related to Tony DeLellis. They were usually asking about my grandfather. Still, I always said: "Yes, all of them."

Every time we were at my grandparents' house, I ran to the shelf where Papa's bronzed shoes and leather football helmets from the 1930s were displayed. I loved imagining all the things those shoes had done to deserve their place. Everyone handled them with care and respect, even the grandchildren—my sister, brothers and I and our posse of boy cousins. We were generally more prone to knocking over lamps, breaking windows with errant fly balls or getting into fights, but we stood stock still when we held Papa's shoes or helmet. They were our family treasures.

Of course, we only cheered for our local teams. If the Dodgers, Lakers, Kings or Rams were playing, my family put the game on the television during dinner. Once in a while, we splurged on tickets to a game. In the years when my dad was still working to grow his father's business, that was a big deal. We would drive the back roads to Dodger stadium in the Chavez Ravine just a couple of miles away, all decked out in Dodger blue, ready to binge on peanuts, Cracker Jacks, and Carnation chocolate malts. Those are some of my happiest childhood memories.

When it was time for baseball try-outs, I heard people say: "Girls can't play baseball."

When I tried on a set of football pads, they said: "You can't play football."

But there was one sport I could play.

My mom says when I was four years old, I started begging to play soccer after watching my brother Tom play on his team. I had to wait until I was five. She says Tom started playing in the backyard with me while I waited that long year. And then, one magical day, I remember I was finally on a field with a ball at my feet and everyone was smiling at me.

———

The first team Katie and I played for had both boys and girls. It was called the Little Rascals, and our dad was the coach. It was all I wanted: to be in a game, in my own uniform, running around kicking the ball in the sunshine—soccer mattered so much to me from the very beginning. It was my first love and my first source of pure joy. It was like someone had suddenly turned on all the lights in my life.

Competing in sports was also the beginning of a new relationship between me and my father. Soccer offered me a new opportunity to please him and capture his attention, which I always desperately craved more of. I wanted us to be able to relate to each other in that way.

Katie and I were good, even among the boys. But the Little Rascals team was the first and last time we ever played with boys officially. If lines existed designating the certain things boys could do and the certain things girls could do, our family followed them faithfully. As soon as there were enough girls to field a few teams, we played for the Strawberry Shortcakes and the Unicorns.

But I was happy. I have a very early memory of getting carried off a field once after scoring a winning goal in a game at the end of one of our first seasons in the local youth league called the American Youth Soccer Organization. The AYSO, as the league was called, was founded in Los Angeles in 1964 with the philosophy that "Everyone Plays" even though they didn't allow girls until 1971 but I didn't know that then. From that moment on, I was absolutely *addicted*. Soccer surpassed my previous favorite activities, including the time we spent with our grandfather, playing in his office as farmers came in and out to discuss business, or listening to him laughing over platters of pasta and meat at Little Joe's downtown with his friends who called us "Tony's little twins." Being the hero in a soccer game was the best feeling in the entire world. I was always hoping to feel that sequence of feelings again: anticipation, adrenaline, focus, confidence, success, joy, pride, accomplishment, love and appreciation.

Soccer was also a way for my sister and me to connect. We were identical twins, so people expected us to be the same, but we were not. My mom taped a card to our refrigerator that said "Geniuses thrive on clutter" and, even though I knew she did not think I was a genius and there were six of us in the house, I knew the message was for me. I liked things messy—or at least I couldn't stop them getting messy—and that card was her way of telling me she accepted me and my untidiness. Katie, in contrast, kept everything she owned neat and in order. She liked to wake up early; I liked to sleep in. She liked pink roses, bows in her hair, and skirts; I wore jeans or shorts with t-shirts. One year I was obsessed with my Halloween costume. I had picked out a Viking costume. It was surprisingly well made. The set included a plastic chest and back of armor, a cool round shield, a sword and—the best part—a silver helmet with horns. It was just my size and I wore it all the time. Around that time, a woman we knew from England referred to me as "the cheeky one." I thought she was calling me cute.

When we were six, Katie gathered up a few of her belongings from the bedroom we shared and moved into the guest room of our house. She didn't ask permission and she didn't discuss her decision with anyone— least of all me—in advance. One day she was just gone. Not long after, she pointed at the threshold of her new room, which was decorated with beautiful white furniture handed down from our grandmother, and told me I couldn't cross it.

Except for a brief, experimental "gifted and talented class" in elementary school, we were placed in different classrooms at school, too. Everyone in charge seemed to agree that we should be "individualizing." At the time, I didn't understand why we couldn't be in the same class once in a while, the way we were with our other friends. Although I delighted in irritating Katie—it may have been my kicking her mattress from the bottom bunk of our bed that drove her to flee our shared bedroom in the first place—I also yearned to be close to her. By continually agreeing to the recommendation that we be separated, I thought my mom wanted us to be kept apart. I thought she wanted us to try to be even more different than we already were.

Our differences became more pronounced as we got older. Katie picked out her clothes carefully for the next day every night. I took to wearing my own kind of uniform, plain and simple, so I wouldn't have to consider my clothes at all. Katie fixed her hair in the mirror every morning. I stopped brushing mine. In fifth grade, she was voted Best Singer, Prettiest

Smile, Prettiest Eyes, and Best Actress. Clearly, actions had consequences. It seemed reasonable because of my personal hygiene and fashion choices that I was not in the running for any of the "looks" categories, but I was still surprised by her nearly clean sweep. I was also surprised at the one award we shared (along with a super-smart and cute boy named Darren): Most Likely to Succeed. I did a double-take when I read it in the little paperback yearbook for the first time, and then immediately wondered if the teachers had cheated and added my name out of pity for the loser twin. The problem was, even though I wanted the awards she was getting, I had no idea how to keep up with her in any of the categories, especially that shared one. Katie seemed to already know what success was; the only path I saw to it was on a soccer field.

I also noticed that the other girls in school seemed more like Katie than me. Having an identical twin who was so different—and, it seemed to me at the time, in many ways better—than me only added to the anxieties I was starting to feel about myself. Katie was living, breathing proof that I could do better.

Our parents weren't pleased with our diverging paths in school. Katie made study sheets and flashcards and stayed up late doing homework in her room. I resented the expectation of teachers that I would do as I was told. I turned in my homework if I could complete it easily, and didn't bother trying to learn concepts that weren't a cinch. I began to think *Why should I do more?* People wanted us to be different: Katie wants to be the good student; I'm happy being the soccer player. It seemed like a perfect division of labor to me. An easy way to tell us apart. Plus, I was feeling another social delineation at school. It wasn't cool to be a nerd. And I wanted to be cool.

Rather than study, I preferred to play in the backyard with Tom, who showered me with positive reinforcement and made me believe I was good at everything. Although he was four years older than me, he spent hours teaching me every sport he knew, including how to throw and hit a softball. Poor kid, he would have loved it if I had taken to it. His favorite sport was baseball, but his efforts were wasted trying to get me to love softball. I was little and so were my hands, and the softball was large and heavy. I wanted to hit the smaller, harder ball, which felt so much better coming off the bat and was so much easier to catch and throw. I was already in love with soccer, where boys and girls played the same game with the same rules and the same ball. I didn't want to be different. I wanted to do everything the same as the boys.

Tom also taught me other very important lessons outside of sports. He was the most loyal and honest person I knew, and he impressed on me that those things were more important than anything else. He also set an example of inclusion for me—he had two best friends, one African American and one Native American-Mexican American.

But sometimes even people I admired couldn't persuade me to follow rules. In seventh grade, my pre-algebra teacher—a man I respected—graded our homework on a scale of one to five, giving every student unlimited chances to correct an assignment and turn it in for full credit. Even though I loved his bold, different system, I simply refused to follow it, preferring to stick with my original score, which wasn't often a five. At the time, I didn't understand my own obstinance. I think part of it was that I was embarrassed to admit I wasn't getting it on the first try the way I thought the other kids were.

I knew I had inherited an aversion to authority. It was Tom who actually witnessed it, but I remember it like a scene from one of our favorite television shows like CHiPs or The A-Team. My father jumped out of the driver's seat of his car and yelled his way out of a traffic ticket. "There's no way you could know how fast I was going!" he roared at the cop, shoving his finger toward the officer's chest. And it worked.

Whatever the reasons, at the end of the year, my math grade reflected my decision not to exert any real effort, and my teacher recommended that I repeat the class. My parents called me into the family room for a private discussion. Sitting there facing them for a talk wasn't a common occurrence so I was nervous.

"Susan," my father said. "Your math grade this year was unacceptable."

I looked at my mom, who offered no relief.

"It's just that we know you can do better," she said.

My father nodded.

"We know that you're capable of the same academic achievements as your sister."

My mom took a piece of paper out of a manila envelope and placed it on the table in front of me. I saw my name at the top, right there in black and white below the bold-faced header: Intelligence Quotient. While I looked at the numbers, which were meaningless to me, my mom pulled a second piece of paper from the envelope and placed it next to the first. They were identical: the headers, the numbers, everything except, of course, the names.

Ohhh shit, I thought, but I was so shocked I couldn't speak, which was fine, as it turns out, because my parents weren't waiting for me to speak anyway.

My mom collected the papers while my dad spoke again.

"Do you understand what this means, Susan?" he asked. He paused for a moment. He only used my full name when I was in trouble. "You are just as smart as your sister, which means you are capable of getting the same grades."

He gave that a chance to sink in before he dropped the bomb. "As long as you keep up with her in school, we will leave you alone. If you decide not to work hard, then we *will* make your life *very* difficult."

I knew my father wasn't bluffing. No one tested my father without facing the consequences. After that, I did try harder in school, but it was a constant uphill battle for me. It was always a very close call whether my grades would be near enough to Katie's for me to stay out of trouble.

———

Even as I began to identify as a soccer player, I didn't have anyone to look up to in the sport. Katie and I were good, but we had no one to emulate. Tony had never played and Tom had picked baseball. And I didn't even know there was such a thing as professional soccer. My family watched football, baseball, basketball, and hockey.

The first time I remember seeing soccer played by anyone other than little kids on a field in front of me was in 1981 when the movie *Escape to Victory* came out. The film starred Michael Caine and Sylvester Stallone and told the story of a group of prisoners in World War II Germany whose escape plan revolved around a propaganda soccer match against a team of Nazis. I found out that my sport had a deep history in other countries in the world, and casting Sylvester Stallone (famous for playing the sports icon Rocky Balboa in the Rocky movies) as an American interloper and opportunist, informed me that the image of the American hero that I'd been taught to admire was not necessarily how the rest of the world viewed Americans. I didn't want to be associated with American interlopers or opportunists. I wanted to be considered one of the real players, one of the insiders. And the first time I watched Pelé changed the game for me and deepened my obsession with the sport. Seeing the way he played taught me that the game didn't have to always be about being the fastest or the strongest on the field. It could also be about being the most magical. I was suddenly desperate to be that good.

Katie was driven in life. She had more all-around ambition than me. She worried about making mistakes, and beat herself up over small things. I thought of myself as more relaxed. I just wanted to be outside in the backyard, firing shots at the house until my father broke down and bought me a bounce-back net. When I needed something new, my mom made up drills for me, like dribbling around the edges of our backyard.

"Now do it with the other foot," she'd yell. Then: "Now go the other direction."

But we were making it up. There wasn't a way to see more soccer, and I'd never even considered yet if any grown-up women were playing soccer. There were some powerful women athletes on television, like in the Olympics every four years or in tennis. I really liked Steffi Graf and the gymnast Mary Lou Retton. The 1984 Olympics in Los Angeles made a huge impression on me. The whole city was talking about sports. The news was watchable. Mary Lou Retton was front and center of every update.

But my everyday sporting heroes were all men. I had my first crush on Dodgers first baseman Steve Garvey. *So* handsome. My favorite baseball player was Fernando Valenzuela. He had the most beautiful, bashful way of acknowledging his adoring fans when they erupted in applause every time he came to the pitcher's mound. The Lakers were a plentiful source of inspiration too: when I was a kid, we had Magic, Kareem and Coop. But my biggest obsession played on ice: Wayne Gretzky. I studied his footwork and passing and dreamed of one day playing like that on the soccer field, being able to score like he did, seemingly at will. My prized possession at the time was a Gretzky jersey. One Halloween, my friend Henry, who lived across the street, borrowed it so he could dress up as the Great One. He never returned it. I heard he worked for the FBI after college, though, so it's all good.

Everything changed when I was about fourteen. My mom mentioned an article she had read about a sixteen-year-old girl named Julie Foudy, who was rumored to be one of the best soccer players in the country and played for something called the Women's National Team, which I had never heard of. The article said Foudy lived in Mission Viejo, a town about 50 miles south of us, and that she was a central midfielder, like me. I wanted to know more about her but didn't know where to look.

My parents discovered somehow that the path to the National Team was through an organization called the US Youth Soccer Olympic Development Program, or ODP, which divided the country into state and regional teams that funneled talent up to the National Team. My dad drove Katie and me to a set of try-outs. We both advanced to the next level to play for Southern California, but we had been placed on different teams. I made the "A" team and Katie made the "B" team. In my mind, the results were fair: she was the student; I was the soccer player.

I'll never forget the first time I got to put on the Southern California ODP kit. They gave us a yellow-gold shirt with official patches stitched onto it and blue shorts and socks. Wearing the California blue and gold— representing my beloved state—filled me with more pride than my little body could contain. By that time, life was beginning to make a little more sense to me. My dad ran things at home, Katie excelled at school, but I had the soccer field. And if I never felt quite in sync with the girls at school, that was OK too. I had teammates. We were friends and warriors, just like my dad and his Stanford football teammates had been.

———

I did have some other female heroes before Foudy: I loved to read about Queen Elizabeth, Amelia Earhart and Sally Ride, the first American woman to fly in space. The day Papa asked me what I wanted to be when I grew up, I answered I wanted to be an astronaut. After he laughed at my answer, I noticed that he didn't laugh at Katie when she said she wanted to be a doctor. I worshipped my grandfather, and not just because he had been a football star. He was funny and handsome and known for his outgoing personality and the stories he told about the days he spent dancing for money on pool tables while his father—my great-grandfather —sold his homemade wine. His laughter told me that my dream was too big. But he'd also once given me an autographed black and white photo of himself in the prime of his football career, signed with the message, "Shoot for the stars! Love, Papa." So which was it? Dream big, or not?

I admired my grandmother, Nana, too. She had taught grade school while Papa was still figuring out his career path and before my dad and aunt were born. If I happened to be at Nana's house—just a few blocks from ours—when her Social Security check came in the mail, she would show it to me and say: "You know, I was a teacher." I could tell how proud she was of the checks and that made me proud too. I understood that they held something beyond monetary value for her.

And yet, my dad didn't want my mom to work. She had been raised by a single mother in a tiny town in rural western Connecticut, had had the imagination and worked hard enough in high school to put herself in a position to attend Stanford University all the way across the country, earned a degree in Latin American studies and later worked for the Peace Corps in Bogota, Colombia. But, after she married my father, she never worked for her own paycheck again. The college degree and a marriage to a man who would always provide for his family was the freedom my mom needed. But I couldn't help worrying that she had given up her dreams. She mentioned to me only once when I was in high school that she had an unfinished novel under her mattress. I liked that dream.

If I had any doubts about how my father viewed a woman's role, he made his feelings much more explicit around the time I was starting high school. We were at Nana's house, sitting at her sunny kitchen table where she had so often shown me her Social Security checks. She and my father were discussing who would take over the family business, and Nana suggested my sister or I could run the company. I sat up straighter in my seat, feeling her belief in me. But my dad's response was quick.

"I'd never give my business to a girl," he said.

I loved our origin story—our own version of the American dream: immigrants working hard and trying to make something for their children and grandchildren. Hearing that wasn't an option for me because I was a girl was a double blow. I don't know if Katie ever heard my father say something like that. If she had, she didn't let on. She continued to get up early every morning to read the financial news with him at the breakfast table.

———

I never doubted that my dad loved me, or any of us. He told us all the time. He kissed us every morning when we woke up and every night before we went to sleep. He used to tell us stories about how, when we were babies, he would hold our hands in his and stare at them—in awe of how amazing they were.

My parents didn't know they would have four children. After they had my brothers and my mom got pregnant again, they didn't realize she was carrying twins until the day Katie and I were born.

"Your heartbeats were perfectly in sync," she would say when she told the story, which I never got tired of hearing. "Every time the doctor put his stethoscope to my belly, he only heard one."

My mother knew she was bigger than she had been with either of my brothers—she couldn't get out of a car without someone's assistance —but she never suspected twins, and neither did the doctor until after Katie was born. When the doctor asked my mom how she felt— she was still catching her breath from delivering Katie—she said her stomach felt harder than it had after my brothers were born. The doctor examined her.

"That's because there's another baby in there!" he announced. And out I came, nine minutes later—a runt at four pounds fourteen ounces.

My dad reported the news to his parents, who at that point had five male grandchildren. "There are two babies!" he yelled from the phone in the hospital room. "Two girls!"

Then he called my mom's mother, far away in Connecticut. "We have twin girls, Dorie," he said with tears in his eyes.

"Oh, goodnight!" she answered and, according to her version of the story, got so woozy she had to sit down.

My dad showed his affection in physical ways. We had nice thick carpet in the "fancy" living room, which we really only used for Christmas. And wrestling. On school nights after we finished our homework or on rainy weekends, my dad would challenge all four of us to a wrestling match. We'd push back the furniture and then have at it, throwing our tiny bodies against his with glee, shrieking when he dragged us back to him by an ankle or wrist. When we got too old to wrestle each other, he would lay down on the floor and ask my sister and I to walk on his back, letting our feet push around the bones and muscles.

The first time I saw my dad beat someone up, I was eight or nine, eating Fun Dip in the stands while my brother Tom played baseball. Tom was pitching, and my dad wasn't happy about the calls the umpire was making. Before I knew it, he was in the umpire's face, and the other team's coach had come out of his dugout.

"You want to take this to the streets?" the umpire screamed at my father, which was a mistake. My father did, in fact, want to take the discussion out to the street.

I don't remember if anyone else in my family was with me in the bleachers. I don't think I moved from my seat. I remember glancing over my shoulder to see the punches being thrown, and then I went back to dipping the white chalky stick into the packet of artificially colored and flavored sugar as if nothing was happening, as if I wouldn't be going home and sitting down to a normal, homecooked family dinner with one of those men after the game.

I was playing in the backyard the second time. Our house was being renovated and one of the workmen had apparently gotten grout on the new carpet in the upstairs bathroom. When my dad came in to check on his progress, he found the man pulling the ruined threads of carpet —which he knew was new—up with pliers. I heard yelling and came around the front yard to see my dad dragging the man by his shirt into the street. Our house was on a steep hill. My dad stood uphill from the man, looking down at him. The workman didn't stand a chance.

It's a strange thing to feel pride and fear at the same time.

———

When it was time for Katie and me to go to high school, our parents took us out of the public-school system and enrolled us at an all-girls Catholic school in nearby Pasadena. My parents are devout Catholics—we went to mass between soccer games on Saturdays and Sundays no matter where our games were, sitting in the pews in our sweaty, dirty kits, sometimes unable to kneel during prayers because of our banged-up knees.

Paving the way before us, Tony and Tom were enrolled in an all-boys Catholic high school after middle school as well, although my father had chosen not to put them at his alma-mater, Loyola High School. When I was old enough to wonder why, I felt sad for them. I assumed they wanted to go there like I did. I'd heard so many stories from Papa and my dad. It sounded like the most special place in the world, a place where students were respected for their intelligence and their athleticism. If I couldn't go there because I was a girl, I wished I could have at least heard all about it and experienced it through my brothers.

When it was our turn to switch from public junior high to Catholic high school, I was not happy about the transition. The high school chosen for us was much smaller than the public school and there were no boys. There were seventy girls in our freshman class. The school building was enchanting though. It was an early-twentieth-century mansion purchased for the Society of the Holy Child Jesus in 1950. Everything about it was fancy but the uniforms were stiff, pastel-colored button-up, collared dresses. I'd been fighting wearing pink dresses my whole life—fighting wearing anything different than the boys, fighting being told what to wear at all—and these were uniquely terrible, although I'll admit they grew on me. For one thing, it was a relief to not be mistaken for a boy anymore. I tried to have a thick skin because I was so stubborn about my clothes, but I had to admit it was tiring being different to the other girls all the time.

The most vivid time I was mistaken for a boy was during an outing with Tom. I was about twelve years old and was wearing my favorite sweatshirt that did come from the girls' department in the store but was not girly. It was a yellow and army-green geometric pattern with maroon circles. I also had a very short haircut, almost shaved on one side and a little longer on the other side. A storekeeper referred to us as "boys." Tom looked at me, bemused but wary. He'd always been considerate of others but he'd also been bullied as a kid because of his two front teeth, so he always tried not to joke at someone else's expense. As he waited to see my reaction, the look on his face—concerned but like he was holding in a laugh that tasted disgusting in his mouth—made me laugh and we walked out of the store, cackling. The assumption wasn't offensive. I knew I was in a gray area between the girls and the boys and if I wanted to stay there I had to be ready for it. So even though the uniforms were forced on me, I did feel relief that I looked like everyone else.

The other thing that helped me get comfortable in those dresses was that we were allowed to wear a pair of boxer shorts underneath. It might sound weird but it worked. Some of the classrooms in our school were small, originally meant to be small bedrooms, and desks didn't fit so we sat on the carpeted floors, cross-legged. The shorts under the dresses provided more freedom of mobility and modesty. Other people didn't care if their underwear might show so they didn't wear them.

When we arrived for ninth grade, most of the girls there had been friends since kindergarten. It wasn't an easy time. I worried about who to sit with at lunch until the middle of my sophomore year when I met two girls who also came from outside the traditional feeder schools. I noticed they each had their own unique edgy style too, a bit rock and roll. Romi and Heather were both in my daily fifth period study hall, and we ended up whispering a lot about music instead of studying. Tom had helped me develop my musical taste, and Romi and Heather had similar tastes: U2, Led Zeppelin, The Smiths, The Cure, Depeche Mode, New Order, Duran Duran, The Go-Go's. We solidified our friendship at a Jane's Addiction concert at the Irvine Meadows Amphitheater. The late eighties and early nineties was a great time to be a music-loving teenager.

My friendship with Romi and Heather grew quickly once we had that daily study hall together. I started to look forward to it. My best friends until then had been from my soccer teams, seeing each other on a practice schedule and bonding over wins, losses, broken bones and bruises. Heather, Romi and I bonded each day by way of a different routine and over a different common love and source of enjoyment. I'll never forget the feeling of listening to the nearly deafening music with them; at that concert, I felt connected to them—and to the crowd around us—in a way I had only ever felt with my teammates. I craved those connections but wasn't great at forming them on my own.

As different as Katie and I thought we were, we always found our lives colliding, even when we least expected it. As with our IQ scores, the first time we took the SATs we got the same score. When we took the exam again a few months later, we both did better—and still got the same total score. Exactly. When the second set of results came in the mail, I had to admit it was definitely weird. I was amused but Katie didn't think it was funny and she stormed off to her room, fuming. I assumed she was upset because she thought she should have scored higher than me.

Meanwhile, Katie had started dating. She tended to have long relationships, mostly with boys of the older-and-with-a-car variety, which was lucky for her. I was still beholden to our mother for rides everywhere.

Our parents had strict rules about how Katie and I could dress or act. We weren't allowed to pierce our ears or wear makeup The rules were harder for Katie, who actually wanted to do those things. We also had a curfew, but our parents didn't enforce it as long as we kept our grades up. Sex was so forbidden it was as if it didn't exist. It was almost never mentioned except for a couple of times when our dad, finding himself with an audience, put my sister and me on the spot: "Hey girls, what's the magic word?"

And we answered in unison as we'd been taught to: "No!"

It never failed to get a big laugh.

Unlike Katie, I was awkward around boys. Early in my high school career, I started traveling more with the Olympic Development Team. One of my teammates was a half-Hawaiian girl named Kim. Her middle name was Pualani, which means heavenly flower in Hawaiian. And she really was. I loved everything about her: the way she played soccer, often airborne and acrobatic; her surfer style; her long dark hair; and the way she didn't back down from anybody. I wanted to be around her all the time. I didn't have a concept of what it meant to be gay or straight at the time, although I had heard people called some female athletes too "manly" or say that they looked "like lesbians." People made homophobic jokes regularly—putting someone down by mimicking them with a flamboyant manner of speech or way of walking. No one ever discussed sexuality in a positive, educational way. My friendship with Kim never became anything more than a friendship, but I looked myself in the eye: I was an athlete, I was more comfortable in boys' clothes, and I could definitely understand an attraction to amazing, badass people like Kim. I was out of the box and I knew it, and I took it personally when people made comments about gay people.

I did have crushes on boys and a handful of boyfriends, mostly for a few hours at a time. One of my first boyfriends stuffed a piece of paper he was holding down the front of my shirt and then ran away laughing.

That was the end of that. I didn't seem able to be in a relationship the way Katie did. I wanted to have fun, but my early relationships with boys weren't fun. In my sophomore year, before our annual Christmas dance, some older girls set me up with the brother of a friend. He was a football player at Loyola, very cute and very cool—clearly too cool for me. I fell for him hard. Sometimes he would come over to watch television at my house. One afternoon, after the boy went home, my dad came downstairs and stood in front of the television, blocking my view. When I looked up, he said: "You know, he's a sex fiend."

I was mortified. It was the first time I heard my dad say the word "sex" and hearing it coupled with the word "fiend" made me instantly sick to my stomach, but it turned out my dad was right. One night, the boy invited me to the guesthouse behind his family's home. When he lay me back on the bed, I realized what he was planning and told him I wasn't going to have sex with him. After that, he lost interest in me. I think he and his friends were in an unspoken race to have sex; by the next weekend, he'd found someone else and accomplished his goal.

I muddled through all these things on my own, not even with Katie. When I got my first period during my first year in high school— impeccably timed to the moment I pulled on my favorite orange bathing suit just before leaving the house to go surfing with a friend and her older brother—my mom grabbed her car keys and told me she would be right back. I paced around the house, watching for her car out the window. I knew about periods from health class, and there had been some very brief, half-articulated acknowledgments among my mom, my sister and me that Katie would most likely be the first to get hers. After all, she was born first and was more mature. (I actually suspected she wanted her period.) But here I was, leading the way for a change.

When my mom returned, she walked into the house, guided me to the bathroom and handed me a plastic shopping bag with a box of tampons and a jar of petroleum jelly.

"Read the directions," she whispered as she gave me a firm push into the bathroom and closed the door behind me.

I was upset that she wasn't offering more help. It wasn't as if we talked about personal stuff like that but I thought this was a serious enough situation for us to be able to get past the awkwardness. Later that day, my first tampon (actually it was my third or fourth, since I had ruined several in my clumsy attempts to insert the little things) came out while I was surfing, forcing me to make an excuse to my friend and her mom, waddle out of the water and cross the Pacific Coast Highway, worried about bleeding down my leg in search of another. I clearly hadn't done it right and I hadn't known that I might need more than one. I wished for a female superhero in that moment—someone to swoop in and save me. This was my welcome to womanhood, but I figured it out. I found a vending machine in the toilets of a fast-food restaurant, went back in the water that day, and never sat out of anything because of it.

———

A new school in a new town was a lot to handle, but a few weeks in to the school year I heard a couple of girls I didn't know yet in my religion class talking about soccer and that helped to make me feel more comfortable. They were trying to talk another girl into playing on the school team that year. I was happy to see that the other girls cared enough to recruit girls to the team, but I wondered if I should be worried that we might not have enough players. I thought to myself, *I really hope they've convinced her to play.* I couldn't wait for the first team meeting.

The physical education at my new school was run by one person. She was a petite woman, very tanned with dark hair and always in tennis attire including a visor. She was the head of the sports department, the equestrian coach, the tennis coach and the physical education teacher. Our school didn't have a field or a gym, so we took the school vans to soccer training at the Rose Bowl complex a short drive away. After Rose Bowl events like UCLA's home football games—during which our field was used as a parking lot—we had tire tracks in addition to normal bumps and divots in the grass.

A few days before our first home game of my freshman season in high school soccer, we still didn't have any kit. No one at the school could tell us where they had been stored from the year before. When we did find them in a box I threw them aside at first as garbage, but one of the older students recognized them.

"There!" she said. "That's them!"

"What... not *those* things?" I said nervously. They were so sad that, if I hadn't been so worried I was going to have to wear them, I would have thought they were funny.

We started to pull them out of the box one by one. There were shirts with different collars, some with long sleeves, some with short sleeves, two shades of brown, at least two different fabrics, some brown cotton, some brown polyester. There were three No.7 shirts, and not a single pair of shorts. The numbers were easy to fix—we used white athletic tape to change one No.7 to a 17 and another to 117—but the shorts were a problem: we just didn't find any. I called every kit supplier in the phone book that afternoon to ask about brown shorts, but no one had any.

The older players—for reasons I didn't understand at first—were adamantly against white shorts, which would have been the only other color that could go with our brown jerseys. When I asked everyone again at training the next day about white shorts, everyone shook their head. One of the older girls standing next to me leaned in to my ear.

"White shorts," she said, giving me a look like I should know what she meant.

I was clueless. Seeing the stumped look on my face, she motioned her head and looked quickly down at my skirt. What was she talking about?

"Oh! Right."

I finally got it: period leaks. I hadn't had an accident like that yet but I definitely spent a lot of time worrying about it. Of course white shorts were a bad idea. I imagined twenty pairs of white soccer shorts covered in grass and blood stains and the big bottles of bleach and the scrubbing they would need to keep them clean all season.

Because there were so many of us it meant that every day a few of us would have our period. It was no longer a monthly individual cycle of worry for me (I never knew when it was coming until after it arrived); now it was an everyday thing that we all shared. Twenty teammates watching each other's backsides, ready to swoop in and take care of each other. I'd wished for a female superhero to rescue me the day I got my first period at the beach, and now my wish had come true. This was it. It wasn't actually a superhero though, it was all of us girls.

Joining that group and the group conversation was life-changing. I remember wishing that every scared little girl just learning about her body could experience this. Whereas my family didn't talk about these things much and avoided a lot of topics, this way felt so much better. I would always be drawn to that openness in other people. I learned how valuable it is to hear about other people's experiences and to realize that we're all going through the same thing. Some of the girls still whispered about it, while others yelled for a tampon from inside a toilet stall before a game. I understood both approaches. Certain topics make people uncomfortable, but I love the louder approach. These things are just part of life, and I saw that they didn't need to be shameful. Of course, it wasn't always as easy as that. I may have been OK following the leaders on my team and being open and carefree about periods and tampons, but it wasn't easy for everyone, and later I would have other things that I dared not even whisper about.

One of the things I learned that year, though, was that some of my teammates didn't wear tampons. At first I had a hard time understanding why they weren't using tampons. Some of them were playing in sanitary pads (some girls were uncomfortable with tampons, some were nervous about the warnings about toxic shock syndrome, and some had moms who disapproved), which explained why they were so worried about leaks and stains. But tampons made it so much easier to play, almost like it wasn't happening at all. Accepting that I was going to have this awful thing called a period every single month for the next forty years and then learning to use tampons and feeling almost completely liberated again was a roller coaster, and tampons were my savior. They weren't a perfect solution to what I considered a problem but, for me, they were the best of the two options available to us.

I also learned that the ban on white shorts carried over to white pants— no white pants when you have your period—and these little "girl tips" went a long way. Being a girl was hard. There were so many things to worry about, but having all these girls around helped me figure it all out.

In the meantime, we still didn't have any shorts and our first game was just days away. One of my older teammates and I drove to a kit supplier, but we hadn't called ahead and they couldn't provide enough of the sizes we needed, in any color in the time that we needed them. At the same time, the school informed us that we did not have a budget for shorts anyway. That left me scratching my head. No one was going to help us get any kit? When we realized that they really weren't going to help us get new shorts, someone suggested that we buy our own. There was a debate about the cost to everyone, but we agreed that since we were buying the shorts ourselves we could keep them after the season finished. So we decided to buy shorts that we might actually wear again, kind of like the theory of a bridesmaid's dress. We ended up with neon-pink, beach volleyball shorts. In our defense, it was the late eighties. Neon was everything, and in Southern California beach volleyball never goes out of style. I was afraid the nuns at our school would object and someone— quite possibly me—would get in trouble, but we never heard a word about our game-day attire. Possibly because they never attended a game. Still, the nuns must have seen the shorts in the halls after our season finished; we wore them under our school uniforms in lieu of boxers, and it was impossible to miss the neon-pink glow from under our skirts.

On the field, our kit was odd but we were good, and there's nothing like being in a big group of girls who are all proud of looking ridiculous. I wouldn't be surprised if the other teams underestimated us because we showed up looking like a circus. I would have. But we had a strong, well-rounded team of kids with positive attitudes and it helped that we had a remarkably fierce goalie, who was fearless and dominated oncoming attackers on breakaways and stared them down to weaklings on penalty kicks.

Katie and I combined for thirty goals that season. I always knew where she was. We never bickered as teammates. It was so much better than the way we were at home and in school where we struggled to get along.

We made it to the second round of the state tournament that year in our division—the first time our school had made the soccer play-offs in school history. We played our first play-off match against a private school on the west side of Los Angeles; our opponents had very clearly not needed to buy their own shorts. They had real kit and a real field.

The game was extra special for me because Tom, who was attending nearby UCLA, showed up to watch. Late in the game, with the score still tied at 0-0, I turned on the edge of the eighteen-yard box and tried to wiggle my way quickly toward goal but was knocked down by the last defender. I landed on my elbow—I hadn't yet learned how to fall properly with my arms tucked in—and felt a crack in my shoulder. The referee immediately blew for a penalty, but I couldn't get up. I couldn't move and I couldn't breathe. My dad ran onto the field, ignoring the ref's calls for him to stay on the sidelines. He helped me gently off the field, and Tom drove me to the hospital. My parents stayed at the game because Katie was going to take the penalty, then later they met us at the hospital and described how she had drilled the ball into the back of the net for the winning goal. Damn was I proud of her when I heard that. My injury tears that had dried up started flowing again. She could handle pressure, my sister.

The next week we lost in the second round of the play-offs, but our success hadn't gone unnoticed. The following year the school gave us a small budget for new kit, so we retired our pink shorts and chose a red and white kit that would always be in stock, easy to get and easy to replace. And *red shorts*. No one in the school administration ever said anything about the transition to the new colors and eventually the rest of the sports teams at our school migrated permanently to red and white kits as well.

That autumn in our new kit we didn't lose a single game, including in the play-offs. We played the state final on a cold rainy day in front of an enormous crowd. The throngs were not all fans of ours but families and friends of other teams waiting for subsequent finals in different age groups and divisions. That big crowd and the pressure of the moment got in my head. My touches were all wrong and I played my worst game of the season. It was the worst experience I'd ever had during a game. The cold, the rain, the thick mud, all of it got to me. I learned about myself that day; self-consciousness was like kryptonite and made me susceptible to choking under pressure.

I can't take any credit for that win. I was overcome with gratitude that my teammates were handling the other team and making it look easy. They were capable and strong around me and we won the State Championship in the small schools division.

A couple of local newspapers printed articles about our team's undefeated season, the State Championship, and the overnight success of the soccer team at our high school. One of them mentioned Katie and me —the identical twins who had scored 73 goals between them in their first two years of high school. Because of Tom, who taught me that getting an assist for a goal was the greatest honor, I never cared about that number, but Papa clipped the articles out of the papers and took them to his office to show his friends.

I continued to make my way through the Olympic Development Program. The ODP coaches spoke an advanced soccer vocabulary that I couldn't get enough of. I loved the precise and clean soccer being played, but my favorite part of the ODP was still meeting girls who were as crazy about soccer as I was. Riding on a bus full of girls who shared my biggest passion was always my favorite place to be.

———

I was an aggressive soccer player, a style of play I adopted to please my dad. My father studied electrical engineering at Stanford but he downplayed his intelligence, always referring to my mom as "the smart one" in the family—I suppose not too different from the way I thought of Katie as "the smart twin." The one thing he didn't mind bragging about was his toughness. He loved to tell the stories of his Stanford football team.

Sometimes he would demonstrate the proper way to "pop" someone with the correct part of the shoulder on an unsuspecting dinner guest or a young football player.

I was proud of my father's strength, but also terrified of it. He was never physical with our family in a bad way—the only time I remember my dad hitting me was when he caught me out of bed after bedtime one too many times when I was really little; his swat to my butt as I had just about made it back up the ladder into my bed sent me tumbling into my top bunk—but knowing his strength was always sort of lurking beneath the surface was unnerving.

On the field my dad preached "reckless abandon." To him, there was no such thing as "too aggressive." He kept himself apart from the other parents on the sidelines and screamed for me to "HUUUSTLLLE, SUUSANNN!" No matter how hard I was playing, I played harder when I heard him yell. I slid in for tackles without any regard for my body, was booked for fouls and threw a few elbows to win a ball.

If my sister received the same from the sidelines, I don't remember. Katie was a striker. She was quick and fast, more of a finesse player. I played in the central midfield. It was my job to win 50–50 balls out of the air and then make sure we retained possession, whatever the cost. I could handle my father's outbursts when they were directed at me, but I didn't like it when he got into it with referees or other parents.

In the summer after my sophomore year in high school, our club team was invited to play in a national championship tournament in La Jolla called the National Cup. We brawled our way into the finals where we were scheduled to face a team led by a girl named Shannon MacMillan. We had some very good players on our team, including a striker, Erin Martin, who would later be called "the closest thing to Wayne Gretzky that prep girls' soccer has ever seen." Martin went on to play at Stanford, where she set a record for scoring four goals in a single game and was the league's (at that time known as the Pac-10, abbreviated from Pacific 10) Player of the Year. Still, MacMillan (who later played for the US Women's National Team and was inducted into the US Soccer Hall of Fame in 2017 alongside

Brandi Chastain) was widely touted as the best soccer player in the state at the time. It was a big opportunity. We had a lot to prove.

We played defensively for much of the first half, trying to hold our own. The game was rough; I had been bumped off the ball and to the ground at one point and felt a sharp pain in my wrist but it would have to wait. Just after half-time, I got beaten on a pass right up the middle and found myself chasing after their central midfielder. She was my responsibility so I had to get to her before our center-back needed to step in and leave her own player unmarked, which was too dangerous—a two-on-one situation right in front of the goal—to even think about. So I did my best to catch her and then dived in for a slide tackle a little farther away from her than I would have liked. I missed the ball and got her legs, and she went down.

When I stood up, the ref pulled out his red card and snapped it above his head. I couldn't believe it. Fouls by the last defender between an attacker and the goal are grounds for a red card, but I wasn't the last defender. And I hadn't been issued a yellow card, which would have warranted a red card on a second offence. A red meant I was out of the game and our team would be competing against Shannon MacMillan's team with only ten players for the rest of the second half.

"What the hell, ref?" I heard from the sidelines. I didn't need to look over to know it was my dad. Cringing, I turned to the ref to try to smooth things over.

"Please, sir, with all due respect, a red card?"

"Second offense!" he replied in a loud booming voice.

I walked off the field in a daze, not yet processing what he'd said. My teammates offered supportive calls in the background.

"It's OK, Sooz!"

"Let it go!"

"We got this!"

When I passed my sister, she reached out to pat me on the back, and that's when it dawned on me: the ref had confused us. Katie had been given a yellow card early in the game, which was very out of character for her. At the same time, my dad—who was filling in as head coach because our actual coach had been delayed by car trouble—realized what had happened too.

"Hey, ref! They're twins!" he shouted. "Ref! *They're TWINS!* She's not the one who had the yellow card! *There are TWO of them!*"

Our goalkeeper coach realized it too. Normally calm, he tried to explain the mistake to the referee, but the ref refused to listen—he was already feeling threatened, which made it impossible to simmer things back down to a calm conversation. The situation was going in the wrong direction. Our two coaches continued their now heated pleas with the official from the sideline until the ref approached them both and flashed his red card at each of them in turn. I felt sick. If I hadn't gone in for that risky tackle, if my sister and I didn't wear No.2 and No.12, if we hadn't worn matching ponytails that day, if I had intercepted the pass instead of letting her get away from me, if I had been playing better and harder the whole game—I wouldn't have been sent off and neither would our coaches.

With both coaches sent off, we suddenly found ourselves without anyone in possession of a valid coach's pass. The ref determined that we would have to forfeit the game. I felt the weight of the whole team, all their eyes, all their parents' eyes, all the effort and expense that everyone had made for years to get to this moment. We would lose without even getting to finish the game.

And then I saw my mom. She was running onto the field and waving something in the air.

"Sir!" she called in a calm but firm voice. "Excuse me, sir! I have a pass!"

I held my breath as she reached the referee and showed him something in her hand. She had a league pass, which let her handle arrangements for our team at tournaments and other administrative tasks. As they spoke, I saw both of their bodies relax before he went across to talk with the opposing coach. They agreed to let my mom step in as our coach. The game would go on. With me on the sideline, and our two coaches off the field, play resumed.

The other team pounded us, trying to capitalize on their player advantage. MacMillan hit the crossbar twice and shot wide on two other attempts. There must have been a guardian angel on our side. We were able to hang on to our lead and we won the game to win the US Club National Cup.

I slept the whole way home, in awe of my mom for stepping up to save the day. The next day, she and I had some rare alone time as a doctor put a cast on my broken wrist. She was usually so busy with the four of us and running things like parent-teacher associations, holiday bazaars, Halloween festivals and handing out coffee and donuts after church on Sundays, so it was nice to have her all to myself for a little while.

———

Our high school soccer team had a revolving door of coaches. First we had an Englishman who I think got hired because of his accent. Then a couple of dads stepped in, including mine. My dad's short tenure went worse than expected. He started talking about running plays like an American football team, dividing up the field into a grid by colors and numbers. We didn't let him come back. The other dad was the best coach we had but he left after his daughter graduated.

Luckily for my sister and me, our parents had found another team for us to play on. It was called a travel club team. Travel club teams weren't like the AYSO teams—we had to try out for the first time and there was no requirement for equal playing time or that every player who wanted to play would be included. The team was called the Foothill Strikers and the coach, Bob Mendoza, knew soccer inside out and played with a fun flair. He was the first adult man I saw in person who actually looked comfortable running at pace with the ball at his feet and could demonstrate the skills we needed to learn, like the placement of a good cross from the corner, for example. He had grown up playing the game. He was a soccer player.

Bob was loud and gregarious and always positive. Our training sessions were intense; we worked hard but we also laughed and had a great time. It was the first time I got to be on a team with an intimidating warm-up—

the kind of super-organized pre-match drills that an opposing team sees before a game and thinks: *Oh shit, we might get our asses kicked today.*

Our coach's love for the game was tireless and he encouraged us to try the new skills that he taught us during training in games, letting us know it took a few times feeling the real pressure and nerves of a game situation to get it right. He assured us that was normal and that we needed to keep trying and encouraging each other to do the same. Most of the teams we competed against came from much larger clubs that had boys' and girls' teams of different ages competing under the same name, but there wasn't yet a big club anywhere near us so we were a single team with parent volunteers overseeing all of the accompanying administrative duties. Yet Bob put together a very good team and the parents all enjoyed each other's company. My dad said that was the secret ingredient of that team.

All the while, my parents were holding out hope that one of their kids would get to go to Stanford. Tony hadn't applied. Tom had a chance, but didn't get in. They didn't expect my sister and me to get in either—and they weren't alone: our high school college guidance counsellor laughed when we told her where we were applying. But my parents wanted us to try anyway. I didn't understand at the time, but I'm sure my parents hoped soccer might help. I didn't know how college admissions worked. I definitely didn't understand that sports could be so valuable but neither did our college guidance counselor.

In the summer after our sophomore year, they surprised us with the news that they had signed us up for the Stanford soccer camp. We were both ecstatic. The coach in charge of my group for the week was Mary Harvey, the first-choice goalkeeper (and Foudy's teammate) on the women's national team who was about to fly off to China for the first FIFA Women's World Cup. All day long, we played soccer on Stanford's beautiful training fields, with the smell of eucalyptus trees wafting over us on the cool breeze. During our free time after dinner, we stayed up late in the common room, watching and talking soccer. It was the most soccer I'd ever seen and the most soccer talk I'd ever heard in my life. They had piles of VHS tapes: soccer analysis, lessons on the fundamentals, match tapes, highlights tapes, you name it. There wasn't enough time to watch them all. The other campers—both boys and girls—rattled off the names of European professionals the way I knew the Lakers and Dodgers. I heard the names AC Milan, Manchester United, Chelsea, Real Madrid for the first time. Any time someone scored in one of the matches on the tapes, the fans of that team ran around screaming "Goooooooooaaaaaaaaaal!" as loud as the television commentators did.

One boy at the camp in particular caught my attention. His name was Matt Stauffer. All I knew besides his name was that he was from somewhere on the East Coast and that he was very serious about life in general and soccer in particular. He wasn't using the evenings at camp to meet girls the way the other boys were. In fact, the only time I heard him talk about girls was when someone asked him to make an appraisal of our performance on the field the same way he did for the boys. He pinpointed who had the best skills, he recognized talent and fitness, and he always made a special point to recognize creativity. I wanted to hear that he thought I was the best, but he didn't. I thought I might have had an outside chance, but toward the end of the week he made his pronouncement matter-of-factly: "Alyze is the best female player here."

I respected his assessment fully and nodded my head. I understood his choice. Alyze played with me on our club team and she *was* that awesome. She was unassuming and lethal, like Rose Lavelle is today, and she was the most dedicated athlete I knew. She invited me over to her house once to hang out and I spied the set-up she had in her little backyard where the grass was worn out from her working on her footwork, and I knew she ran every day in the steep hills in the real-deal heat of the San Fernando Valley. That was how she spent her free time. She talked about high school and the college standardized tests with confidence and she was excited and ambitious about college. Her mom even influenced me, asking me about school and what I liked the best. Alyze was a student-athlete. She was the first person who inspired me to think I could also be both, that I didn't have to only be one or the other. I had been keeping my grades up just enough so I didn't get in trouble, but I never wanted other people to call me a student. Now I thought maybe I could reclaim a little bit of the "student" label that I'd assumed was only for Katie. Alyze was also really fun to be around and absolutely adorable with shiny black curls, gorgeous brown eyes, and freckles. When I was around her, it felt a little bit like a crush. I was desperate for her affection and attention and not sure what to do with myself when I got it. But it was still a very binary world where girls liked boys and boys liked girls and that's just how it was.

Not long after the Stanford camp, I traveled to Oregon with the ODP team for the Nike Cup. After one particular game in which I had a diving header that hit the post, coaches from schools all over the country came up to introduce themselves to me. I couldn't believe some of the insignias on their shirts: Duke, Dartmouth, Harvard. In my wildest dreams, I had never considered myself Ivy League material. Every chance I got, I mentioned that I had a twin.

"You should see my sister play, and her grades!" I'd say.

In the fall, the phone started ringing. The coaches wanted to talk to us, not our parents. I didn't know what "empowerment" was yet but, in retrospect, talking to coaches after the game and then continuing to speak to them on the phone—feeling in control of my future—was the first time I remember feeling it. I knew I had done my part to catch the coaches' attention, but I also appreciated that it was my sister's innate work ethic and the high academic standard she had set for both of us that made those schools even a remote possibility.

Jen, our goalie from the Foothill Strikers who was a year older than us, had just applied and been accepted at Stanford. That was a turning point because it meant that it could actually happen to people like us. She reported to preseason at Stanford at the end of the summer and the rest of us went back to high school. I called her that autumn.

"How are you doing?" I asked.

"It's going great! I love it!" she said.

"What is Foudy like?"

"She's just as amazing as we thought. But, once in a while, I do actually take the ball off of her feet."

Wow. Just wow. I always had to peel the phone away from my face at the end of our conversations because I was listening so closely.

Katie and I were invited to visit a few schools as soccer recruits to meet the players and see the facilities. We decided that a visit to both Dartmouth and Harvard would be once-in-a-lifetime experiences that we had to try to make work. My parents did just that, turning the trip into a family holiday to visit our East Coast family.

Katie was excited about the Ivy League schools from the beginning. She had exchanged letters all year with our grandmother in Connecticut and they had fostered a tight bond, so she was excited about being a drive away from her instead of a 3,000-mile flight.

A cousin of my mom's threw a family reunion while we were there. We got to see our grandmother and our East Coast cousins, uncles and aunts, including dozens of relatives on my mom's side of the family who we had never met before. We heard stories about that side of the family who came to America from England in the mid-1600s. That changed my image of us a lot. We had deeper roots in American history than I'd known and I felt a validation for the connection to England I'd always felt but could never explain. One of my mom's cousins upon hearing that we were going to visit Harvard told my mom: "Well, that would be great for the family."

It turned out that being on a recruiting visit to a school meant getting personal attention from one or more of the current players and being introduced to the team and around campus as a recruit. When we arrived on campus, we would meet up with the coach at his office and then get matched up with a current player as a host. Each time one of our hosts introduced us to another student on campus as a soccer recruit it felt like my self-esteem was a sandcastle and someone was slapping heavy solid handfuls of wet sand onto the foundation. Nothing had ever made me feel more special.

Dartmouth's campus was dripping with charm. The sports department offices and hallways, the soccer team's dressing room, dorm rooms and classrooms had a musk that made sense—it smelled like an Ivy League school. Dartmouth's soccer coach at the time, Steve Swanson, was a very genuine and kind person who we connected with easily. My sister and I both loved the happy aura in and around Dartmouth and the girls on the team, but it was 14°F and snowing when we sat in the stands to watch the team play a mid-season match. That. Was. *Insane.*

Harvard was a regal and fascinating place, and for my sister I think it was love at first sight. I loved it too. Harvard Square felt like a picturesque town in a foreign country, like I imagined Cambridge in England looked like. Terraced townhouses and buildings with tons of historic charm and cobblestone streets.

We met Tim Wheaton, Harvard's coach, in his office on campus and then several of the girls on the soccer team took us to a dormitory version of the wacky seventies game show *The Dating Game* in the Leverett House dining hall. One of the Harvard women's soccer players was putting questions to the three contestants, the three "bachelors." The rest of the girls on the team were in the audience and had moved chairs from other tables so that they were all sitting in a tight bunch, some squeezing three girls onto two chairs. They clearly loved each other; their sisterhood was unmistakable. They were like the spectators at a tennis match, all turning their heads in unison, their laughter bellowing through the formal dining hall.

I had never seen anything so creative or funny. The girl in the game was clearly a leader—confident, smart, funny. I imagined that if I went to Harvard I could be like her. I wanted to be one of them. But my Stanford blinders were strapped tightly around my head and I put them right back in place. Besides, I thought to myself, this was all just a lovely lucky exercise. I probably wasn't getting in to either school, but definitely not Harvard.

It was around this time that we heard a rumor some college admissions departments had strict policies regarding the admission of a set of twins. We heard that twins who applied to Stanford were accepted or denied individually and that twins who applied to Harvard were accepted or denied as a pair. Alarmed, I feared that my sister would get in to Stanford and I would be totally rejected, and that if we didn't get in to Harvard, she would point out that it was probably my fault.

When we got the call inviting us to visit Stanford as official soccer recruits, the coach said: "We would love to have you come on an official visit."

It was overwhelming. Giving my parents the news was the most exciting moment. They both got tears in their eyes. After the phone call I felt like I had swallowed a big gulp of air that situated itself nervously in my belly. My heart raced, and kind of itched, leading up to the trip.

My former teammate, Jen, was scheduled to be my host. Halfway through the first day with Jen, I found myself standing face to face with a smiling, oh-so-adorable-in-person Julie Foudy. Coach Andeberhan and Jen had arranged to surprise me. And they succeeded.

Julie Foudy was my idol but she was also the team's ambassador, their celebrity and their jewel. My heart swelling, she introduced herself to me as simply "Julie." Hopefully I said something intelligible and sincere to her like, "Wow, Julie, it is such an honor to meet you. I've looked up to you since I was thirteen." But realistically, I might have been catching flies in my mouth.

She led me away from my grinning friend to her biology class, talking to me energetically the whole way: "I have biology right now. We're getting our midterms back. And after that we'll head down to the field for practice."

I relished every second of our walk and the hour I got to sit next to her in the dim lecture hall. I was wildly proud to be associated with her. Midterms were passed back at the end of class. Foudy openly showed me her B+, saying: "I'm applying to Stanford Medical School."

I was star-struck now on an academic level as well. It was the way she openly and unapologetically excelled. I still believed that being a nerd wasn't cool, yet her confidence and clarity made her immune to that negative peer pressure. It was liberating to think I could be that way too.

After her biology class, Foudy took me to watch the team's afternoon training session. I was in heaven watching them play in the perfect Palo Alto weather. They were working on their structure from the back, switching the point of attack, swinging the ball around their back line with increasing speed. It was lovely; my friend Jen dishing out the ball from goal and Foudy's elegance dictating the easy flow from side to side. It was by far the most exciting day of my life. I prayed I would get in too so I could play with the amazing women in front of me and be as confident and ambitious as Foudy.

Later that autumn of 1991, Julie Foudy, Mary Harvey and many of the other original icons of the US Women's National Team like Mia Hamm, Brandi Chastain, Kristine Lilly, Joy Fawcett, Carla Overbeck and April Heinrichs, traveled to China and beat Norway in the final to win what I thought was the first FIFA Women's World Cup. Decades later I found out that FIFA wouldn't allow that first women's championship to be called a World Cup, as they were worried it would tarnish the image of the men's event. But at the time I didn't know anything like that was going on. There was no online portal or website for up-to-the minute information about the National Team or women's soccer. I don't know if the games were shown on television but we also didn't have a way to record them. Besides hearing bits of information at games and training, any information I got was from a sports newspaper called *Soccer America* when it came out a week or so after the events.

Michelle Akers had scored ten goals in the tournament, including the two goals to win the final. I didn't see her play myself until the next women's World Cup in 1995, when my mom took me to Sweden to watch the tournament. Akers was the tallest, strongest, fastest, most technical female soccer player I had ever seen. She was one of those people who completely reset the bar of possibilities. I remember feeling disappointed in myself that I hadn't heard of her before. I had to find a way to follow this team.

Back home, the college counselor in our high school was telling people that we had wasted time and money with applications to schools we could never get in to. She was very convincing, so I believed her and felt guilty. And our dad wasn't impressed by the Ivy League schools.

"I don't give a crap about Harvard," he said when my sister told him she would love to go to either one if she got in.

I knew he desperately wanted us to go to Stanford. Our parents had both done well there—my father on the football field and my mom as Queen of the Quad. It was where my parents had met and fallen in love; nothing compared for them.

I asked him one day about how financial aid works for college. I'd been so naive, not thinking about it before then, and now the time was getting closer. He didn't really want to talk about it, but I was worried. I knew that paying for college was unaffordable, not to mention paying for twins in college, but I hadn't known about the recruiting process or that I could have pursued schools that might have offered me scholarship money. I didn't know the system. I kept asking him until he finally told me: "Susan, we won't qualify for financial aid."

That didn't seem fair to me. How could people be expected to pay so much for college, especially for twins? So I found some financial aid paperwork in our college counselor's office at school, filled out as much as I could and brought it to him one night as he was sitting in his chair with his beer at his side. He realized he was going to have to spell it out for me.

"Susan, we won't qualify for financial aid because I make too much money now."

"Oh."

I took that in for a long time, standing there with the paperwork in my hand, like a statue. I finally understood that all of his intensity had been paying off that whole time. He had started with nothing and figured out a way to be ready to pay for all four of his children to go to college. I wanted to understand his incredible path from where he started and what he'd accomplished. It felt odd that I'd been so in the dark about his business's success. But he was so modest. Thinking back, there were big clues that I'd missed completely—like a beautiful watch for my mom on her forty-fifth birthday. I hadn't noticed that my father's company had grown up faster than me.

But there were other big things in my life happening too. Romi was the first one of us to be old enough to get her driver's license. Her father walked out of his little Italian village with a donkey when he was eighteen years old, dreaming about opportunities in America. He put himself through college and electrical engineering school in Northern Los Angeles and opened his own engineering firm, finding a niche putting in grids of light poles in the large shopping-center car parks that were being paved everywhere around us to accommodate our car culture. I overheard my dad say once—and I thought about how it also applied to Romi's dad's business—that the best businesses were the ones where you were selling something that people always needed more of. So Romi's dad could afford to buy her a car and he was happy to do so.

Her dad bought her the cutest little white, two-door Volkswagen convertible. We loved that car so much, and the freedom it gave us was exhilarating. There were moments where that car and all that freedom created danger and we were too stupid to see it. Most of the time we escaped without consequences, but there were stories of others who did not. Like the story the girls at training told me about a group of kids packed into a small car driving too fast that flipped near the Rose Bowl, killing a young teenage girl who had gone to our high school. Another time we stopped for burgers and fries at a popular place very late at night, finding ourselves in a different scene from the one we were used to in the daytime but we stayed, not smart enough to change course. We sat down with our food at one of the outdoor tables. We had our change on the tray next to our French fries. A very large boy walked up to us, took the money off the tray and walked away. We sat there wondering what to do and then we just got up quietly and went back to Romi's car. When we sat on the seats we both realized that we were sitting on sharp pieces of broken plastic. On the dashboard of the car where the radio had once been was now a rectangular hole with multi-colored wires hanging out. That was the last time we parked the car with the top down, and we started being a lot more careful about where we went late at night.

On weekends, we zipped around between house parties with the top down, talking to people at stop signs and blaring out music, picking people up, dropping people off. One chilly night, Romi and her boyfriend were sitting in the front seats and I was sitting in the back seat. We were parked talking to friends outside a party about where to go next. A group of boys came out of the party and walked to one of the other parked cars. We recognized a couple of them. Somehow one of them ended up in the back seat of Romi's car with me. I don't remember how that happened. We closed the roof of the convertible but didn't turn down the music, and Romi's boyfriend leaned in to kiss her. I stopped trying to talk to them and turned my head to avoid seeing them make out. The boy in the back seat with me started talking but he was slurring his words and making no sense. He was drunk. Not just drunk though, I realized.

Even though he was really out of it, he could tell what they were doing in the front seat. He stopped babbling as he assessed the situation. He looked at them for a while and then he looked at me. His expression changed and he started moving in my direction. I thought he would stop. He continued moving over and tried to kiss me. No one had ever come at me like that before. He smelled like alcohol and he was sweaty. I blocked his face with my arm, still believing he was going to stop. He never hesitated or acknowledged in any way that I wasn't reciprocating. The back of the car suddenly felt like a trap. It closed in on me. I had retreated as far as possible, and was now pinned up against the inside of the car. There was no way out without totally freaking out and embarrassing myself, Romi and both the boys. The scene flashed through my mind of me causing a big scene and making everyone get out of the car. At the time I felt like I had put myself in a bad position again. I believed the blame and shame would land back on me. This boy would definitely say I'd overreacted and acted like a loser, and everyone would hear about it at the next party. The thought of all that seemed like the worst fate imaginable so I stayed quiet and reassured myself that I was going to be able to handle it. But his shoulders seemed to expand in size and blocked my view of the other side of the car. I realized then that he was much bigger than me, and his giant hands were everywhere, all at once. All over me. He was grasping and groping. He just kept going, getting inside my shirt, and when I blocked him there he moved with an unexpected quickness between my legs, yanking on my underwear. I remember concentrating on not making any noise. Every second that passed I was in disbelief and growing shame. I'd been too proud to make a scene and now I was too humiliated to make a scene. I was sweating at that point, telling myself over and over: *He's going to stop. He's going to stop. He's going to stop.* He did finally stop, as if he had been exorcised. His shoulders deflated, his expression returned to babbly drunk guy and he moved back to the other side of the back seat and slumped back to sleep. All so quietly. He looked like a regular guy. Like nothing had happened. He'd never taken off any of his clothes. I started to straighten myself up carefully and silently. My wrists were sore. I pulled my bra back over one of my breasts that he'd got to, and I fixed my underwear and pulled my skirt down. I was so grateful Romi and her boyfriend in the front seat hadn't noticed. Among all the frantic thoughts running through my mind was a question: *How does someone enjoy that?*

I didn't tell anyone. Not even Romi. Not my mom or my sister. Certainly not my father. Part of me wasn't sure anyone would have believed me, anyway. I imagined their faces scrunched up with doubt: "Why *you?*"

I had never doubted my strength—that's where my pride came from: faster than the boys and picked first for teams in elementary school, playing through broken bones and blood on the soccer field. My father had taught me to be strong, so I was strong. My grandfather had laughed at my crazy dream; my dad had told me I couldn't run his business, but until I was in the back seat of that car, I had never felt *weaker.* Now I knew the truth: we *are* weaker. I felt stupid. All of my power left me. It broke me in half.

———

One day in the spring of our senior year, two letters came in the mail from Stanford University. My mom, sister and I were all home when they arrived. Katie handed mine to me, but I was too terrified to open it. Instead, I held my breath while she ripped into hers.

My mom and I stared at her, waiting for a sign. We watched as her hand went to her mouth, her face flushed red, and her eyes filled with tears. My own face felt hot in sympathy. I tried to see the shape of her mouth under her hand but couldn't. Finally, she looked up.

"Accepted!" she yelled.

Eyes welling up, I grabbed the letter from her hand to read it for myself: "Congratulations! You have been accepted to the Class of 1996!" I was stunned.

My chest tightened when I realized I was still clutching my own letter. It sounded like my heartbeat was being broadcast on a loud speaker in the room. Not breathing, I opened the envelope and pulled out the single sheet inside, trying to read through the words as fast as I could. I saw the ones I had been afraid to hope for: "Congratulations! You have been accepted to the Class of 1996!"

A chill went through my body, a mixture of surprise and relief flooding my veins. My mom and sister wrapped their arms around me, and we hugged for a long time.

"Oh wow," I said. "Oh wow, oh wow, oh wow."

I hadn't even finished saying "oh wow" when the doubts started to push their way in and flush everything else away. I couldn't stop it. Was I good enough to play at Stanford? Was I good enough to play with Foudy? Had I only got in because of my parents? What if my dad drove 350 miles to see me play, convinced all his buddies to leave the Stanford football tailgate to join him at the women's soccer game, and then I sat on the bench and never got in the game? What if I sat on the bench for an entire season? I was overcome with self-doubt but kept my feelings to myself. My parents were so excited I didn't want them to know I was feeling anything but happiness.

A day or so later, another pair of skinny letters arrived, this time with the Harvard crest on the envelope. Katie and I brought them into the kitchen where our mom was drying the dishes. She stopped when she saw what we had in our hands.

"Open at the same time?" I asked Katie.

"OK," she answered, exhaling deeply through her mouth.

We kept our eyes on each other as we opened the envelopes and then read the letters as fast as we could. Again, I was holding my breath. I could feel a heavy weight pressing on my shoulders—my sister's dream of attending Harvard.

Oh my god, I thought as I read my letter.

We looked up at each other at the same time, trying to read each other's expression before revealing our own. I caught the tiniest micro-expression of joy on her face before she smothered it with worried sympathy, and that's when I knew: we had both got in to Harvard.

I threw my arms in the air, jumping up and down. My sister and mom joined in and we danced like lunatics in the kitchen in front of the fridge with the little card my mom had put up so long ago: "Geniuses thrive on clutter." My mom had accepted me for who I was. Now apparently Harvard had too.

Katie didn't waste any time. As soon as she could, she filled out the paperwork and rooming card. She was going to Harvard. She was so certain about her future. I had to remind myself I wasn't going to Harvard. I was going to Stanford. That was *my* dream: to follow in my dad's footsteps and to play with my hero, the girl in the article my mom had cut out of the paper for me so long ago. I filled out my paperwork for Stanford, and we put it all in the mail.

That night, Katie came into my room for the first time in years, braving the glasses of gelatinized milk and plates of moldy peanut butter and jelly sandwiches. I cleared enough space on the floor for us to sit quietly facing each other, cross-legged, knees touching. We talked for hours, remembering what it was like to be close off the field like we were on it. We cleared the air about a lot of things, including our identical SAT scores.

"I wasn't mad at your score," she said, shocked that I had thought she was. "I just wanted my own score to be higher. I was disappointed with *myself*."

As soon as she said that, it made sense. Of course, she was disappointed in herself—she was *always* disappointed in herself. She would never be happy with her score on anything until it was a perfect score. That's the way she was, and I had always secretly admired her for it. It made me rethink my interpretation of seventh grade math when I was embarrassed to admit that I wasn't getting it on the first try. She hadn't been getting it on the first try either, but she just never gave up until it was perfect.

After we talked, I realized for the first time that I could decide to stay with my sister. No one was going to make us go to different schools or separate us into different classes. Being near her felt more important all of a sudden than going to Stanford or pleasing my father or, as crazy as it sounded, playing with Foudy.

I bailed on my dream for hers, just like that, but it didn't feel like bailing. I told myself I was *choosing*. But in the back of my mind there was more going on. I think the fear of failing at Stanford was scarier than the fear of failing at Harvard. And on the flip side, the unknown of Harvard was so much more exciting than the world at Stanford that we already knew so well.

I called the Harvard coach the next morning and asked: "Can I still come?"

He said yes. He still gives me a hard time about it to this day.

My mom was OK with our decision. She was from the East Coast and knew what the Harvard name meant, even if my dad didn't. He, on the other hand, didn't try to hide his disappointment. We knew how much he loved Stanford and how strongly he had hoped we would play soccer there, but it was something more than that. He started desperately trying to convince us to change our minds, and I had never seen my father desperate. One day, during an argument with our mom about our decision, he let the reason slip, yelling: "*Marion*, they are going to meet someone from back there *AND STAY!*"

It was sweet that he wanted so badly to keep us close but I was shocked that his biggest fear of us going to school on the East Coast was that we would follow in our mom's footsteps by falling in love and never coming home. He was getting a little ahead of things. Besides, I had no intention of staying on the East Coast. I was a beach kid, a sun-worshipper. I hated cold weather. This was just a four-year adventure.

When his pouting didn't sway us, he resorted to bribery. He had bought us a car to share for our last year in high school—a cute little red BMW that he'd agreed to buy because of its advanced airbag system— but, since the transportation of choice for Stanford students on campus was scooters, he offered to buy us each one if we went there. That almost worked on me. I pictured myself driving around the beautiful, manicured streets of the Stanford campus, to and from class and training, past Memorial Church, waving at Foudy.

Nevertheless, Katie and I stood strong. Or I stood strong. Katie never wavered.

The year flew by. At our high school graduation, my beautiful sister wore pretty little white flowers in her hair and knocked the salutatory speech out of the park. I had an unfortunate haircut, wore the required dress that didn't fit me right, and had an unusually bad breakout; it was a dismal sort of hat trick. Still, the summer was ahead of us with endless days of soccer and nights of pool-hopping.

There were still a few more things to take care of. At the top of my list was that thing called sex. I still hadn't had it and everyone else had. One day, it hit me that I couldn't show up at college still a virgin. That would be mortifying. I was casually hanging out a lot with a local boy. He was fun and adorable and easy to be around. We actually had really great conversations. I knew I could trust this boy. He was a virgin too and I knew he respected me, so I decided to take ownership of the decision rather than let my body be the subject of some boy's raunchy quest.

One afternoon I took him to my room and we took care of it. That's how it felt to me—calculated and transactional. He was sweet and kind and I was glad it was done—one less thing to worry about when I was starting my new life in college. It didn't even cross my mind that maybe that wasn't fair to him.

I packed my favorite soccer ball. That's all I remember that was definitely in the back of the Explorer we loaded up in the driveway in front of our house in August 1992, when Katie and I were leaving for Harvard. My soccer ball and a lot of camping equipment. And not a lot of winter clothes.

Tom had offered to drive us across country. The consummate older brother—he had once kicked a boy out of a party who dared to say something disrespectful about us—he wanted to be nearby to protect us.

He was also looking for an adventure of his own. He had just graduated from UCLA, had dreams of becoming a poet, and had set his sights on getting a job at WordsWorth, a famous bookstore in Harvard Square where he hoped he could work to make ends meet and be around likeminded book lovers while Katie and I went to school and played on the team.

Except for our father's apparent concern that we would be married off and living permanently on the East Coast within four years, our parents were less worried than our brother. Their stress seemed to have been whether we would get in to Stanford, not how we would fare when we left home for Harvard.

At least one other member of our family was afraid for us. I remember taking a near-frantic call from my dad's sister on the day we left. She knew "the twins" were leaving for college, and she'd timed her call perfectly.

"Please, please, please don't have unprotected sex!" she said sternly out of nowhere toward the end of our conversation.

I snorted, then tried to recover. It was important advice and her delivery actually made it more poignant. I appreciated that it took guts for her to say that to me. I loved her for it, but I didn't know what to say back.

"Thank you?" I offered. It was all I could think of to say.

After we said a very awkward goodbye, I laughed to myself, appreciating her attempt to help me. Despite my one instance of uninspiring sex in my bedroom, no one normal had spoken to me about safe sex before. In our high school, the nuns were in charge of health class and, to make their case for abstinence, had showed us slides of vaginas infected with genital warts and other sexually transmitted diseases—an effective deterrent strategy for all of us not smart enough to look away.

I was thrilled Tom was going with us. As excited as I was for the next chapter in my life, I had no idea how I would fare so far from home. I'm not sure how Katie felt, but she had always been more independent than me. And if she ever did need help, she was more likely to rely on a boyfriend than on me, Tom or our parents.

My dad felt the significance of the moment.

"I have one thing to say," he said as we were piling into the car. "Take a few minutes to stop what you're doing every once in a while and feel and see everything around you. Try to take it all in. Otherwise it will all go by too fast."

His sentimental words made the moment feel monumental. As we took our places in the car (I had been assigned the tiny available corner of the back seat for the first leg of the journey), I felt a brief twinge of panic—that cold-sweat feeling you get when you're strapped into a roller coaster and wish you could change your mind and get off but it's too late.

We were off. And, just as fast, the panicky feeling was gone. I have never felt freer than I did during that road trip in that car with my brother and sister. If we wanted to turn left, we turned left. If we wanted to turn right, we turned right. We were free to get lost—and we did, in epic fashion, driving for nearly 100 miles in the wrong direction once before we realized what we had done and began screaming at each other in the confines of the car. We camped each night, pulling up between giant RVs, making friends with whoever was around us, eating hot dogs, soggy hamburgers, chips and all the other junk food that accompanies road trips. One night, outside Yellowstone, we cooked an entire pot of pasta over our campfire and then promptly spilled it in the dirt as we tried to drain it.

"It's fine!" I yelled, hungry and tired. "Let's rinse it off and eat it!"

But Tom and Katie refused, so we trudged back to the camp store in the dark for more and started all over again.

We traveled the northern width of the country in a little over two weeks. We listened to a lot of loud music and we had conversations we'd never had before. I got up the nerve to ask Tom something I'd always wondered about: I asked how he felt about going to St. Francis instead of Loyola. He said our dad had explained it to them. Our dad had told his sons that he felt Loyola was too far and dangerous a drive. He'd been right about that too. My brother Tony had crashed a car on his way home from high school even on the easier, shorter drive.

We stopped at the sacred Bighorn Medicine Wheel at the top of Medicine Mountain in Lovell, Wyoming, part of a massive Native American archaeological site. Tom told us that he had been there on a road trip the previous summer with his best friend, Aaron. Aaron had been one of Tom's closest friends for years. He was a sensitive person like Tom. He was the kind of person who befriends his best friend's adoring little sister.

Aaron's father was Native American, but he hadn't seen him in years. That had partly been the purpose of their big road trip—to see if they could find him. Sitting at the top of the mountain that afternoon, Tom told us that during their big adventure across the country and back, they had succeeded in finding Aaron's father, a Vietnam veteran. They'd found him living in a trailer six miles north of Priest River, Idaho, on a dirt road. His trailer had no running water or electricity, and he'd had some of the toes on his left foot amputated due to frostbite the previous winter. It was clear that the boys had been shaken by the experience.

Tom had always easily shrugged off the dogmatic approach of the Catholic church—and our parents—toward religion (my parents worry that children who aren't baptized will suffer in purgatory for all eternity) and had instead embraced a variety of spiritual beliefs. I was grateful that Tom had brought us there and shared that painful story with us. I felt concerned for my brother and his friend and a connection in my heart to that special place, a tenderness that I assumed my parents felt in church. I hoped the Medicine Wheel might have had a healing influence on the boys somehow.

We stopped to see Mount Rushmore, the all-white, all-male monument we looked up to without yet questioning it, and then in one epic day in Chicago we went to the top of the Sears Tower, caught a Cubs game at Wrigley Field, and then saw the Violent Femmes open for the B-52s at an outdoor amphitheater not far from our campground in our version of Ferris Bueller's day off.

I chalk it up to youthful ignorance that I was able to enjoy that experience without any anxiety about what was to come. I tried to run during our stops at campsites but was afraid to go too far in that pre-mobile phone era, so I was doing barely anything to maintain my fitness. In hindsight, two and a half weeks on the road as I was preparing to join a Division I soccer team was a mistake. But I didn't think anything of it at the time.

PART 2

THE HARVARD YARDS

Under Ivy League rules in place then, freshman athletes weren't allowed to train with their team until courses had officially started, which meant we weren't allowed at preseason. So, when Tom dropped us off outside Harvard's gates at the end of August, Katie and I joined the rest of our incoming freshman class for a longstanding tradition called the First-Year Outdoor Program. We had a choice of community service, hiking or canoeing. Katie went hiking; I chose canoeing, spending a week in Maine, sleeping on the ground under a plastic tarp with a bunch of other Harvard freshmen that I barely knew, eating canned tuna and getting eaten alive by bugs. I loved every minute of it. Every single person on that trip had the most amazing story of how they'd got there. That was always the best thing about Harvard—the exceptional people from places I'd never been, with stories I could never imagine. The Northern Lights appeared late one night after we had cleaned up dinner at camp on the edge of the remote lake. There was no moon. The swirls of green and neon flares were so vivid it was impossible to believe they were natural. I remembered what my dad had said and took it all in as best I could.

Back on campus, Katie and I were whisked apart again. We had been assigned to dorms on campus as far away from each other as physically possible. Most of the freshman dormitories were in Harvard Yard, the original center of the historic campus and main thoroughfare for student life. The 25-acre area is enclosed by a stately brick wall with intricately detailed wrought-iron gates so famous they had a book written about them called, appropriately, *The Gates of Harvard Yard*. Katie's room was in the Yard. She had been assigned to Massachusetts Hall. Built in 1720, the hall predates the birth of the United States and once housed the Continental Army. John Adams lived there. So did John Hancock and Samuel Adams.

Not me. I was assigned to a dorm called Pennypacker. My building was not inside the Yard. In fact, before it was purchased in 1958, it wasn't affiliated with Harvard at all. It was an apartment building later converted into student housing. While my sister was marinating in Harvard's historical marrow, following in the footsteps of revolutionary war heroes, I was living across from the Hong Kong, a smelly, sticky-floored dive bar famous for its cheap Chinese food and giant "scorpion bowl" of alcohol punch. It was kind of perfect.

Still, my three roommates—a writer from Florida, a DJ from Maryland and a theater lover from nearby Concord—and I piled into a fourth-floor suite and made the best of it. By the end of the autumn, we had made t-shirts for ourselves that read: "Top Four Reasons to Party in Pennypacker 45."

Despite my new roommates, I felt far away and out of place. I missed my parents and grandparents. I missed Tom, who had found an apartment in Allston and got his job at WordsWorth and told me he would see me at my games. I missed Romi and Heather. I missed Foudy and Stanford.

I assumed my sister was fitting in beautifully, as she always had. She was taking pre-med courses toward her ultimate goal of becoming a doctor and, within a few weeks, had started to date the senior captain of the men's soccer team. He belonged to one of the more girl-friendly finals clubs (which normally exclude women) so she'd been "upstairs" in the members-only areas of the club during parties, which was a big deal. Sometimes I would see her riding across campus on the back of his scooter, but she was always long gone before I could catch her attention.

My teammate Libby told me one day that one of the players on the men's team was interested in me. He was a sophomore and, unlike Katie's boyfriend, he didn't see a lot of the field. I agreed to go out with him.

I liked him. He was cute with shaggy, curly brown hair and blue eyes. Once we had been dating for a while, though, he wasn't always nice—he made comments about my intelligence—but he was smarter than anyone I'd ever met before so I let it go. He was studying to be a doctor and had been an accomplished violinist. By the time he and I met, though, his violin-playing days were over. He had practiced so obsessively that he had given himself nerve damage in his elbow. While we were dating, he was teaching himself to write with his left hand.

My self-confidence was rattled and I felt like, as some Harvard professors and students were not shy to inform me, I was "just an athlete." In the Harvard hierarchy, I found myself several rungs down from the top of the pyramid, which was the male intellectual elite. Male athletes and non-athlete females were both ahead of me in the hierarchy of Harvard belongingness. I still wasn't sure what I wanted to study, and my weakening confidence wasn't going to help me make a choice. None of my natural interests had been encouraged besides soccer. One day on a phone call with my parents, I made the mistake of talking to my dad about what I was thinking. The conversation was brief.

"I'm thinking about concentrating in English," I said. Concentration was the Harvard word for Major.

"You mean business," he replied.

"What about computer science?"

"You mean business."

When I told him a few days later that I was considering environmental science, he was even more clear.

"That's just dumb," he said. "You should study business, Susan."

I could hear him shaking his head on the other end of the phone. Life was so much easier when everyone let me just concentrate on soccer.

In the end, I took mostly required first-year courses—freshman writing, quantitative reasoning—during the fall semester, but I also took the introductory economics class for my dad, and surprisingly liked it. The law of supply and demand was one of those concepts that was like a "where have you been all my life?" kind of thing. For electives, I took a popular history class about hegemony in the beautiful Sanders Theater of Memorial Hall, which made me feel like I was living in the history I was studying. The building was constructed after the Civil War to honor Harvard alumni who fought for the Union cause, and it felt more like a nineteenth-century church than a classroom.

I also took an introductory philosophy class called Alienation and Autonomy, which summed up my freshman year experience pretty well. I felt like I had reached a certain degree of autonomy. I had traveled far from home to attend college, after all, but I was alienated too. From everything I'd known before. From my sister, who I only saw at training. From my brother, who I only saw at games. And from the school itself, which was starting to feel old-fashioned and foreign to me, and—most worryingly—stuck in a time when it was still acceptable to exclude women and condescend to athletes as inferior in intellect. That class struck a chord with me. One of the lectures was dedicated to the belief that self-torture is intrinsic to human nature. The turtleneck-sweater and corduroy-pants-wearing philosophy professor said Harvard students were surrounded by one segment of the population that dealt with this tendency toward self-torture in a healthy way. He asked if anyone knew who he meant. No one did.

"Athletes," he said.

———

As usual, soccer was the highlight of my life. On the day we were finally allowed to train with the team, I was the first one to arrive at the Harvard Square T stop, our designated meeting spot, and from there we walked across the Charles River to get to our training and match-day facilities. Seeing my sister walking toward me instead of riding away from me on the back of her boyfriend's scooter brought tears to my eyes. I'd been feeling really isolated. I couldn't wait to get back out on the soccer field.

At the complex, we were issued with training shorts and shirts and mesh laundry bags with giant numbered safety pins to drop off our dirty clothes in to be washed every afternoon. Our dressing room—small, gray, and smelly—was in the Gordon Track Center. I loved it. I got butterflies every time I punched in the code to get in. It was my new home. My new safe space. And the team was my new family.

Our coach, Tim, wasted no time in bringing us together as a team on the field. He briefly introduced the freshmen and then told everyone to grab a partner. For a second I was worried I would be left out, and I started to move toward Katie, but a senior student grabbed my arm with a big smile. Someone else took my sister's hand.

"Slide tag!" the coach called.

The older girls shrieked with delight as we all lay down on our stomachs next to our partners in the grass for a soccer warm-up I'd never played before.

The introductions continued off the field with the men's team. Each year, the two teams met in the Malkin Athletic Center for a talent show in which the freshman men and women performed skits in front of the players and coaching staff. Our class put a skit together impersonating the coaches and seniors. As I stood next to my classmates, getting in my place for the performance and terrified I might throw up, the junior central midfielder on our team nicknamed Flynnie yelled out: "Floooooozeeeee!"

When I realized she was talking to me, I laughed and blushed. Everyone laughed. We started our skit and luckily all we had to do was keep that laugh going, which was a lot easier than starting one from scratch. She hadn't called me Floozie before that moment, and she has rarely called me anything else since. Like a lot of good nicknames, I wasn't sure about it at first, but I had to learn to love it and was Susie Floozie, Floozie or Flooze from that day on.

Our class—like every freshman class on the women's soccer team before us—was affectionately known as "The Shmennies," shortened from freshmen. We went to training together and to dinner after training together. We carried the cones, water jugs and bibs to and from the field. We collected all the balls and moved goals on demand. In general, if there was a job to do we did it, and if a senior player called we came running.

On the day of our first game against the University of Maine, we jogged in pairs from our dressing room, past the open end of the U-shaped football stadium to our field next to the beautiful brick and ivy-covered buildings of Harvard Business School. No one spoke. All I could hear was the sound of our cleats clattering on the concrete. When we reached the grass, freshly manicured and painted with clean white lines, I felt a rush of happiness and pride. Ohiri Field—named for a Nigerian-born All-American who lost his battle with cancer after helping the men's team win three Ivy League titles—was my first home field. It wasn't a borrowed space that doubled as an overflow car park. It was ours to share with the men's team. There were benches and stands and a loud speaker and a working scoreboard.

My dad's advice came to me. Without thinking, I broke out of our two-line formation and dived into the grass, spreading my arms wide and pressing my palms into the cool blades. Turning my head from side to side, letting the grass brush my cheeks. Fans were beginning to trickle in and the Maine players were beginning their warm-ups. After a nice long moment, I popped back up. I was running to join my teammates on our sideline when I heard my brother's voice.

"Sooz!"

I turned toward the fence and saw Tom standing with his camera.

"Oh my god!" I screamed.

I ran over and hugged him tight. We chatted hurriedly for a few minutes about his apartment, his roommates and his job before I went back to the team for warm-ups.

"Can we have dinner after the game?" I called over my shoulder.

"Yes!" he shouted. "I'll wait for you. Sooz... good luck!"

Our two captains set the tone during pre-match warm-ups and kept us all loose but focused. They chose the music that played over the loud speakers. I wondered how Tom felt about their selections. It was a mix of popular East Coast musicians like Bruce Springsteen and Frankie Valli and the Four Seasons that I grew to absolutely love. I felt like he might think we'd gone back in time. It did feel like that a lot at Harvard.

A few minutes before the whistle, our coach, Tim, brought us into the huddle to call out the starting line-up. My sister and I were both going to start. Noonan, a hilarious half-Swede from Winchester, Massachusetts, was the other freshman starter. I was too nervous to appreciate the accomplishment. Katie was playing up front, as always. Tim had put me at left wing. I'd been playing outside in training but still didn't feel comfortable there. I'd forgotten that Tim had only seen me play in one game and that was at the tournament in Oregon where I'd played out wide. Before that game my ODP coach had asked who wanted to play in central midfield, but I'd been too timid to raise my hand.

"No problem," I told myself when Tim outlined our positions.

But it *was* a problem once the game started. I couldn't get in a rhythm. I was running my ass off and was still always out of position. If I did manage to get behind the defense to be an option for an attack, then I couldn't get back fast enough to defend against the counter. I was winded well before I should have been and, even worse, began to feel invisible— something I had never experienced on a soccer field. I was used to being at the helm of high-scoring wins. Now I had the terrible feeling I wasn't pulling my weight.

As a team, we struggled to put together any scoring opportunities. When the ninety minutes were over, we had squeaked out a 1-0 win but it was without much help from me. I was disappointed, but luckily our older teammates knew to take the long view.

That night, after Katie and I had dinner with Tom, my roommate picked up the phone in our dorm and held it out to me.

"It's for you," she said. "Someone named Flynnie?"

My heart skipped several beats as I put the phone to my ear.

"Hey, Flooze! Meet us at the Grille in thirty minutes!"

I was exhausted and had reading to do but knew better than to say no.

"Yep," I answered. "See you there."

The Crimson Grille was a hub of the social scene for Harvard students at that time, and it was a gathering place for athletes. When I got there, the other freshmen, including my sister, were already huddled outside the entrance. A large man was sitting on top of a bar stool, wearing a gray Members Only jacket and a tweed flat cap. As we waited, the door burst open and Flynnie popped her head out.

"Guys," she said. "This is Dave, one of the owners of this fine establishment. Dave, these are our new Shmennies. Take good care of them."

Dave shook our hands and gave us each a pat on the back as we walked by him, pointing out his coowner Paul inside. Once we were all inside he caught the door just before it closed behind us, and said: "Kick some ass for us this season, OK, gals?"

Inside, Flynnie led us to a collection of tables where some of the senior players were waiting with pitchers of beer and grins on their faces. Then we talked. Or rather, they talked. They talked to us and around us while we listened until quickly we became comfortable enough to share things as well. They wanted to know how we were doing with our roommates and how we were feeling about picking our classes.

Once we started talking, we had a lot to say, and they listened to every word. I told them about my dad and our conversation about what I should study, and they laughed, which made me feel a lot better.

Soon everyone was talking about something called "final clubs." There was a buzz about them. They were a major topic of conversation among the boys we knew—mostly other athletes just by nature of our common schedules and daily routines, walking back and forth to the athletic complex over the river for afternoon training, sharing an equipment and laundry window, and usually sharing dining halls before retiring to homework and bed. The way the boys were talking about the final clubs made me want and need to hear more and I noticed that no one was talking to us about joining clubs. The boys continued to inform us about all the excitement. An extraordinary social life existed at Harvard—that was a relief—but it started to become clear that girls were not included. The core of Harvard society was set up for men and by men.

We heard about the boys finding wax-sealed envelopes slipped under their doors in the middle of the night inviting them to go through a process called "punching." It was a selection process, a series of increasingly exclusive parties. We heard stories about parties in mansions—the image in my mind was of handsome, powerful men in tuxedos, eating lobster and entertaining each other with witty remarks and limericks. I imagined their elaborate feasts: tumblers of expensive scotch, cigars, and them ending the night standing on chairs singing their hearts out unabashedly.

Once in a while I was able to catch a glimpse behind one of the massive front doors of one of the clubs. Each club owned a townhouse in Cambridge. The ivy-covered buildings, the historic and charming classrooms and libraries on Harvard's campus were the most elegant buildings I had ever been in, but they didn't compare to the final clubs. They were the epitome of decadence—a window into another world. They were American versions of palaces and the membership list was full of American royalty like the Roosevelts and Kennedys.

A few of the clubs traditionally included a party in their punch season and the boys were expected to bring a date. We would hear about all the dates and parties in the dressing room before training. I wanted to be invited but was also afraid that the invitation came with an expectation.

Once initiated, the members had access to the clubs as a home away from home, just steps from campus, most with a full-time caretaker and chef. Some excluded girls even as guests; others allowed girls in for parties. On one or two nights that year, I ended up in one of the clubs with friends from one of the men's teams. Late at night, we would sneak into the commercial kitchens for pickles or ice cream. It was like a dream world, but it was hard for me to be totally comfortable there. I always felt like a gatecrasher and as though the price of admission was accepting a place as a second-class citizen.

Later I did hear about one women-only club that had been started the previous year by a few women in a room in one of the upperclassmen houses. I remember feeling a sense of exhaustion for them—catching up to the level of the existing men's clubs with their 200 years of amassing wealth and status and real estate was an impossible expectation—but I admired the secret, bold group of women and would have loved to find a mysterious envelope under my door any morning.

The second game on our schedule—to my total shock—was Stanford. It was like a record scratching in my head when I realized it. How could I have not noticed that Stanford was traveling across the country to play at Harvard that year? What were the chances of that? I kicked myself for not having thought to look ahead at our schedule, but I'd assumed we only played East Coast teams, none of which I knew very much about. As the freshman athletes in the Ivy League weren't allowed to go to preseason, after less than a week of training with the team we were going to face Julie Foudy and Stanford, who had been training together on those beautiful eucalyptus-scented fields for a month.

I felt better as soon as I saw my friend and former teammate Jen warming up to start for Stanford in goal. Recognizing each other from across the field, we ran to meet one another with huge smiles, exchanging high-fives and big hugs and a quick happy chat. Then I spotted Foudy. It was an equal mix of pride and fear knowing I was going to be playing on the same field as her that day, the latter was stronger. The butterflies in my stomach were on the verge of making me sick. She looked comfortable and confident as usual in her position and her role as the leader of the team. I didn't feel any of those things. I felt entirely inadequate. And suddenly self-conscious about our kit that was too big for us and cheap—a batch of t-shirts ordered for both the men's and women's soccer teams.

I was too shy to remind Foudy that we'd met before, so I never approached her. But playing on the same field as her that day was one of the greatest honors of my life—never mind that Stanford beat us 3-0. It was the only loss where I found myself smiling for ninety minutes. I would have loved to play directly against Foudy in central midfield, but being out wide and watching her was fun too.

The season didn't get much better—for me or the team—after that. Tim was consistently playing me out wide. I scored one goal that season, from a penalty. That really hit me. *One goal.* Any assists I had were forgotten because I was so disappointed that I'd only scored once. I felt like I had failed my team. We were losing games and I had failed to turn that around. There were a few highlights—a draw with top-ranked Cornell, a win over the University of Pennsylvania in which Katie had a goal and an assist, a victory over our cross-town rival Boston College—but, at the end of the season, we were ranked fifth in the Ivies, the team's worst finish ever.

Still, we stayed strong as a group, largely because of the traditions that connected us to the teams who had come before us and the teams who would come after us. There was always a sense of perspective and continuity —the idea that we were part of something bigger than ourselves—that made individual losses less devastating and gave the wins meaning and context.

On our first road trip of the year we were heading to Columbia University in New York. No matter whether we had won or lost, the last one on the bus for road trips was always required to entertain everyone else with songs, jokes and embarrassing stories. I arrived for the bus early that foggy morning with my fellow freshmen, only to find everyone else already on board. As we filed up the steps, Tim greeted us with a smile and started to clap his hands. Pretty soon the rest of the team was clapping and cheering too. It turned out that the senior players had intentionally told us Shmennies to arrive late to make sure we were the last ones on the bus.

Before the main event of the bus ride, which was the senior players grilling us about our personal lives, they made us put our right hands over our hearts and swear a simple line of allegiance:

"I, [we stated our names], do solemnly swear total and permanent allegiance to the Harvard Women's Soccer Team with loyalty and team love for all."

It was not to be taken too seriously, but it also felt *really* good. It had power; it felt weighted. We'd gone through a hidden door, earned our way into the club. It felt good to be on the inside of what I could tell already was a very special group of women, something that was forever.

There was another special moment, a beautiful moment, once all us freshmen were done with our interrogations and a vibe in the bus began until the whole bus was soon clapping and cheering for one of the senior players to sing. She was a blonde junior nicknamed Korny. She got up confidently and everyone hushed in anticipation. With a smile on her face, she began to sing the most beautiful ballad. I had never heard anyone sing like that before, in such tight quarters, alone, with actual talent. Her voice was so pure and refined. It was like she was not only soothing us but filling the bus with kindness as she sang. After her last note ended, the bus erupted in applause and cheers, all of us so impressed, inspired and proud of our teammate's talent.

We had traditions on the field as well. Sometimes, Tim ended training with a round of World Cup, my all-time favorite game. The two-on-two tournament started in chaos and ended with a pair of trash-talking champions.

On days when we had enough time to recover before our next game, Tim scheduled tough fitness sessions to increase our stamina and push our mental limits. We ran full-field sprints called 120s and shorter shuttles known as suicides, with agility drills in between. There's nothing like shared misery to bond people together. In training before match days, he eased up, having us focus on footwork and set plays. There were a lot of blisters, a lot of ankles getting wrapped, and a lot of ice.

All the Harvard athletes shared a deep mutual respect. We organized trips to cheer on the other teams, and sometimes those other teams—ice hockey, squash, lacrosse—shared teammates of ours, which blew my mind. That was a new level of superhuman to me: someone good enough to play two sports at that level.

Whenever we could, we attended the men's soccer games, joining in songs along with the other fans: "Olé, olé, olé, olé, Harvard! Harvard!" They were like brothers to us, with a few crushes mixed in. One of their seniors, an engineering student who went by the nickname "Ho" (a shortened version of his last name), invited everyone to his dorm on Monday nights for what eventually became known as the "Monday Night Ho Club." We'd sit around talking and singing the choruses of Pearl Jam's debut album *Ten*, which was on repeat by popular demand.

Sometimes they would tell stories about their coach, and we started to get a picture of the culture of their team. It sounded like he was critical without the constructive part. We felt them getting demoralized. We could all relate—coaches had power over our lives. And players' opinions weren't given any weight. The worst situation was when the coach was not only not a good coach but also not a good person. If you wanted to stay on the team, there was nothing to do except keep going.

Our strongest bonds were with each other. I thought back to who my father's best friends still were: they were his former teammates. He spoke to them and sought advice from them. One of them was his lawyer, another his financial advisor. We didn't see them that often because they were spread out around California, but they were helping him through life. And when we did see them, it was like seeing our real dad. We got to see him through their eyes, his peers who loved him and poked fun at him and called him deprecating, endearing nicknames. My teammates were more than my friends—just as my father's had been. They were family, my role models, my fellow warriors, my comrades. And my teammates were trying to awaken me to the fact that we were in a battle not just on the field.

The older girls on my team told me a little bit about the law called Title IX, or Title Nine, and how it had made our team and most of the other women's teams at Harvard and other universities in America possible. They invited me to make phone calls with them to raise money for an organization at Harvard called the Harvard Radcliffe Foundation for Women's Athletics (HRFWA, pronounced "herf-wah"), which was founded in 1981 by Patricia "Pat" Henry as the Radcliffe and Harvard sports departments were still merging. Her purpose was to build an endowment for women's sports and incentivize former female athletes to give back to their programs to try to accelerate equity in funding with the men's teams whose alumni bases had been growing and contributing money for generations.

I walked through the hallways in the sports department, looking at the framed black and white photographs of every varsity team in Harvard's history and noticed that there were so many more hallways full of men's photographs. They went back deep in history to teams wearing increasingly antiquated-looking uniforms, much older than the age of Papa's memorabilia. In contrast, the women's teams didn't go back much further than us. I hadn't known our history was so much shorter. It dawned on me that the women's team was *less than twenty years old*. The juniors and seniors on our team encouraged all of us to join them in Women Appealing for Change, a group organized by some of the women's lacrosse and field hockey players that was planning a boycott of the final clubs because they were so obviously discriminatory. My Harvard teammates were trying to help me understand—and feel ready to challenge—the inequality on campus and beyond but I didn't feel like I had any power yet. I didn't think my voice was important.

They were also teaching me more personal things, like how to take a naked shower in a group setting.

My small Catholic high school didn't have a dressing room or any sports facilities except tennis courts, and the showers in my public middle school were such a relic they weren't even hooked up to water, so I was used to waiting until I got home to shower. We were a private family. Bathroom privacy was the norm. I knew from my recruiting trips that college teams showered together. At Harvard I'd been handed a cookie by a stark-naked senior player in the dressing room like we were at a picnic in the park. But I still wasn't prepared for those first few experiences. Still, after our first training session, I knew the time had come. I stepped anxiously out of my sweaty clothes, trying to hide myself with one of the very small towels issued by the sports department. I could hear yelling and laughing from the shower room next door. I began to panic. My mind raced:

Can I do this?

Don't look at anyone.

Don't think about what you're doing or, God forbid, what you look like.

Everyone is doing it.

You don't have a choice.

Don't be a loser.

My boobs are too small.

My thighs are too big.

I can't just walk around naked!

I look ridiculous.

What if I have my period?

What if I fall over?
Just take a deep breath and go for it!
Go for it!
GO! GO! GO!
Shit, don't look like you're rushing!

The walk from the shower back to my locker with that tiny towel was agonizing. I barely bothered to dry myself off before I started hurrying into my clothes.

I felt a tap on my shoulder and jumped.

"You still have water all over your back," a senior player said. "Don't get your clothes wet because you'll freeze when you walk back over the bridge."

That's when I realized: I didn't need to be scared or worried about what my body looked like or what other people thought my body looked like. When we stripped down in front of each other, what we were really stripping away was shame.

There was more. Our dressing room had a giant green chalkboard known as the "slutboard." It soon became clear that getting your name on the slutboard was actually the highest possible honor and could be achieved in any number of ways: talking to a member of the men's team after training, being seen sitting next to a boy in the dining hall or the library, an actual romantic date the night before, getting spotted going into or out of one of the exclusive male-only final clubs, sharing the story of a terrible date. Being a slut, on our team, meant owning your body and your sexuality proudly, however you defined it.

The top right-hand corner of the slutboard was reserved for the Finemaster, whose identity was kept secret. Each year one of the juniors was chosen to be the Finemaster. The job evolved a little from year to year. Mostly she was responsible for fining players for infractions by writing their name, the infraction and the amount of the fine on the slutboard before anyone else arrived for training. Infractions could be anything from being late to a training session or a team event, forgetting to bring the cones or equipment out to the field or back, forgetting shinpads, telling a bad joke, things like that. The Finemaster was in charge of collecting enough money to throw an initiation party for the freshmen after the end of the season.

The chalkboard was also used for the daily pictogram message. The senior players would quickly put letters, words, plus and minus signs as needed with other symbols and drawings to produce a clever message about how we were going to crush our next opponent. Tim would come into our dressing room once it was ready and try to figure it out. Watching them pull the message together out of nothing, the sound of the chalk on the chalkboard, the giggling and erasing and giggling that went on, then Tim struggling to come up with the meaning—it was our daily entertainment like a recurring segment on a late-night talk show.

As my confidence was growing among my teammates, I was struggling in my relationship with my new boyfriend—or, as Katie called him, "my benchwarmer-neurotic-violinist boyfriend." We were having sex (only after one of the captains had guided me to the University Health Service to get contraception) but I knew the experience wasn't what it was supposed to be. He was critical of my body and was constantly shaming me for being inexperienced. Rather than give up or recognize it as unhealthy, I kept trying to do better.

Toward the end of the season, Tim pulled us all in to announce that Bertie, one of our juniors, had been awarded Academic All-Ivy honors. Everyone clapped and cheered and she laughed her fun-loving, contagious laugh. It was the first time I'd heard of that award. I was constantly being inspired by these women. They were not satisfied to have just got in to Harvard like I was. They had even greater expectations for themselves. They had plans for *after* Harvard too. Smiling, I was truly happy for her. I was impressed and proud to be one of them.

After the season, without the routine of daily training and regularly scheduled games, it became harder to stay in touch with Tom, Katie and the team. Noonan had become my closest friend. Her laugh brightened up every day. Her father was an administrator at Harvard, so she had grown up there and knew everything I didn't. She taught me that before graduating, every Harvard student was supposed to do three things: have sex somewhere in Widener Library, pee on John Harvard's statue in the center of Harvard Yard, and streak naked through campus, which she swore—without convincing me—was a major stress reliever. Who knew Harvard students were so crazy? Noonan made friends with everyone— on every team, in every club, and in every class—and knew where to pick up our varsity club "H" sweaters as soon as we were eligible and where all the best parties were at all times of the night.

After our season, the women's lacrosse coach invited all of us Shmennies to try out for the lacrosse team. She said she knew we were fit and athletic and she could teach us the rest. I never even considered it because I wanted to stay focused on soccer, but Noonan and our other roommates went, made the team and played.

In the spring, Harvard freshmen choose the group of students they will live with for the remainder of their time on campus, entering the housing lottery as a unit. There are twelve undergraduate residential houses for rising sophomores, and on "Housing Day" the results of the lottery are announced by the senior players, who adorn themselves in their house colors and crests and storm the Yard, waving their flags and scarves to claim and welcome new housemates with the most house pride. Currier House residents wear green—sometimes just green speedos; Adams House wear their Adams house black blazers and matching boxer shorts; Dunster House wear furry headband-antlers to represent their mascot Henry Dunster Moose (Dunster residents are affectionately known as Meese); and so on.

I chose to room with Noonan, another freshman teammate and a friend of ours from the field hockey team. My freshman roommates had each other, and my sister chose her freshman-year roommates. My sister and I hadn't lived together since she moved out when we were six so I assumed she wouldn't care. I knew they would all be fine without me, but I still wish I had asked.

I felt like I was finally finding a comfortable place. My future roommates and I met often at Herrell's Ice Cream Shop in Harvard

Square, talking for hours in the windowless vault of the former bank building known as the "fish bowl." Then, winter struck.

I had never experienced even a mild winter—as far as I can remember, all our trips east to see my mom's mother had been during the summer. The winter of 1992–93 was a blockbuster, with long stretches of sub-zero temps and a record-breaking Nor'easter that buried everything in sight and left behind mountains of bright white snow that got covered with a layer of gray soot and stuck around until late spring. Each morning I walked out of Pennypacker with wet hair from my shower. I didn't own a hairdryer— I'd never needed one at home—and with temperatures below freezing, my hair stiffened into icy dreadlocks that made a hissing sound if you squeezed them. My nose hairs became prickly needles; my eyebrows crystalized. I remember realizing that I was going to be seeing my breath for months.

It shouldn't have been a surprise that my sister and I both got very sick that winter—Katie worse than me. One of my roommates gave me a message that she was in the infirmary and, panicking, I rushed to find her. She looked wilted, exhausted and pale. I wanted to crawl up beside her in her hospital bed, to hug her and stay there with her forever. It turned out she had mono and her spleen was enlarged. Luckily, Nana and Papa had scheduled a trip to visit us around that time. Upon arrival, they snapped into rescue mode and bought us each a heavy down parka, snow boots, warm socks, hats and gloves.

When the snow finally melted, the men's team organized an informal kick-about on Ohiri. With a keg tapped on the sidelines, we had a version of the usual pre-match ceremony. We all stood to attention facing the flag as they blasted Led Zeppelin's rendition of the "Star Spangled Banner" on a boombox. We played all afternoon, happy to be back outside on the grass in decent weather.

Except for a few informal "captains' training sessions" there were no real organized team commitments during the spring. We were largely on our own through the summer too, when Tim handed us all a packet of fitness drills and expectations to keep us in shape until preseason started up again in August.

Katie and Tom decided to stay in Boston for the summer and so, having no other plans of my own except to train every day for soccer, I stayed too. Katie was taking organic chemistry as part of her pre-med studies, and I took the introductory chemistry course to keep my option of medical school open too. We had to formally commit to a concentration at the beginning of sophomore year and I was still trying to find a compromise with my dad. Feeling very grown-up, the three of us rented a small apartment not far from Harvard Square in Somerville. But we weren't very good at taking care of ourselves. Meals, for one thing, were a challenge. Katie was trying to lose weight. She had gained weight partially from being sick for so long with mono, and I didn't see her eat a lot that summer except single baked potatoes out of the microwave. I was no better—most nights I ate whatever I could find by myself in the tiny kitchen, wondering where my siblings were. I missed eating in the dining hall with the team.

Apart from classes, and the daily workouts Katie and I put ourselves through at the nearby fields on Tufts University's campus, we were largely disconnected from each other and everything else. Tom worked as often as he could, Katie had a new long-term boyfriend, and my boyfriend had gone home for the summer. Katie and I had decided against playing for a summer league team. She wanted to focus on her class, and I stopped going after the first couple of games. It was hard to get a ride and I worried I might get injured. Instead I walked to the manicured sports fields at Tufts and went through our summer workout packet. I had two goals: to earn my spot as a starting central midfielder and to win the Ivy League Championship. I didn't understand the importance of staying match-fit. I thought I could do everything on my own.

———

Bad things started happening in August when my brother Tom got a phone call that his best friend, Aaron, had set his mother's garage on fire. We assumed it was an accident, but the details were relayed to us that Aaron had been acting erratically for months. He had been admitted to a psychiatric hospital on a seventy-two-hour hold and he was asking for Tom. Tom drove home immediately to be with him. It was disturbing news, hard to comprehend. It was my first experience with anything psychiatric at all—no one ever talked about mental health or therapy or anything like that. I didn't know that someone who was vibrant and healthy could so quickly become dangerous and unstable. How did that happen?

Katie and I reported to preseason a few days later with the rest of our team, including—thanks to a rule change in the Ivy League—our incoming freshmen. We had been nicknamed the "Dark Horse of the Ivies" by the *Boston Globe* and, to celebrate, our captains devised a mock-serious "hazing" ceremony, blindfolding each freshman and taking her into a dark room. There were abundant stories of real hazing going on at college campuses at that time. The look on their faces when they came out of the dark and realized there was nothing serious about it and that they had a not-at-all-ominous temporary tattoo of a horse on their arm was funny every time.

It was the first preseason for us sophomores too but, because we had a year under our belts, our experience was a little easier. We tried to make it more comfortable for the new Shmennies the way the older girls had helped us, except that we did call them Shmennies and they did have to carry all the equipment. I was giddy that everyone was finally back from the summer break and that we were preparing for another season. I couldn't wait to start playing and I was ready to help us win more games.

But first we had to pass our fitness tests. No matter how fit you thought you were, it was impossible not to feel nervous as we walked to the track, and it was weird to see everyone in running shoes, but we tried to smile through it as much as possible. The camaraderie of the team gave us strength and endurance beyond anything we could have had on our own. In the end, no one was left behind especially the two who ran to the nearest garbage bin to throw up after crossing the finish line. We were all pushing ourselves that hard. It could have been anyone.

Despite my lack of significant points the previous season, Tim still had confidence in me. In fact, he had selected me as one of two central midfielders. That was a great day. The fitness tests were over and I was so excited to be in the middle where I felt most comfortable, feeding balls to my sister and everyone else, steering the team from the center. I was looking forward to helping put a lot of balls in the back of the net, to winning games, and to proving myself.

In the first training session on the second day of preseason, I hit a cross with my right foot from the corner flag to the far side of the six-yard box, a long pass I had made hundreds of times over the course of my playing career. As soon as the muscle contracted and before the ball even left my foot, I felt a searing pain tear through my right thigh like I had been stabbed with a knife. The shock radiated through my nervous system, simultaneously up to my brain and down to my toes. Time slowed down. I felt dizzy and saw black for a long, strange moment and then swarms of stars zigzagged in the air. I didn't even look to see where the ball landed. A headache immediately set in; I saw black and I leaned to the left without meaning to. Catching myself, I turned for the sideline and galloped awkwardly off the field to where our trainer was standing.

Tim saw me step out of the drill and yelled: "What happened?"

I shook my head and tried to yell back but couldn't form any words, eventually managing a strained: "Not sure."

I passed my sister and her expression mirrored what I felt inside: confusion and fear.

Our training staff drove me back to the sports facilities on a utility cart. Inside, they asked me some questions and examined my leg and determined I had strained a quad muscle and would be out for four to six weeks. Even though that meant I would miss at least a third of the season, I was relieved at the diagnosis, which seemed much less severe than what I was experiencing. I set my expectations accordingly.

At the annual talent show, our freshmen mocked the captains who had tattooed them just a few days earlier, to all of our cheers. The freshman boys were equally entertaining, making fun of their seniors—but I was unprepared for how disorienting it felt to be taken out of the line-up and training. Instead of training with the team, I spent hours in the treatment room, alternating between electrical stimulation treatment, ice and heat, and when deemed ready, trying to stay fit on a bike. On days when I finished in time to watch some of training, I paced around the field with another teammate who had torn her ACL, both of us counting the days until we could play again. I felt unfit even though I was working out as best I could.

Meanwhile, I assumed my quad was healing because the trainers told me it was. After exactly four weeks, I said I was ready, the trainers agreed, and Tim put me back in the starting line-up at central midfield.

During the warm-up—the most I had run or kicked in weeks—I felt a twinge in my quad but ignored it. This was the moment I had been waiting for.

I didn't even make it ten minutes past the starting whistle. My quad let go on the first semi-long pass I attempted—a standard 15-yard ball to a teammate running up the sideline. This time it felt like the muscle ripped right through the middle and snapped up into a ball at the top of my thigh. I tried to play through it but I realized I was crying and all I could see were stars again. This time, I couldn't seem to control my right leg very well even when just walking. Lowering my head, I dragged myself off the field at the next whistle.

The trainers said it would just take a couple more weeks. I wanted that to be true so I went back to my physical therapy routine, telling myself to work harder. Every day, I got to the treatment room early for physio and then went out to watch the team train or play. But I felt more and more isolated, especially from my sister.

Katie was playing her best soccer yet. She was excelling in her courses in the history of science. I had chosen environmental science as my concentration—to my dad's dismay. Katie was dating an incredible guy; despite the sympathy I had shown for my boyfriend's elbow injury, he was less interested in me since my injury. And Tom, my go-to source for self-esteem and reassurance, was gone, struggling on his own at home, trying to help his friend.

For the next match in which I was cleared to play, I changed my strategy. My plan was to avoid using my right leg for long balls at all.

Once, I used my left foot to lift the ball over the defense, putting Katie on a breakaway to goal. I pushed to accelerate, to support her from behind the way I always had, but I couldn't catch up to her. The field had never seemed so long.

I watched from downfield as she took her shot, narrowly missing the goal.

"Good try, Katie!" I screamed, hoping she heard me. She seemed miles away.

The feeling of not being able to run—of not being there for her—became a recurring nightmare. I would dream that I was in a game, feeling that urgency to get to the end of a pass, and my feet would be stuck to the ground.

And that became the cycle, paying my dues in the treatment room, convincing everyone I was fine, getting clearance to play, and then re-injuring myself. the end of the season—after making appearances of just a few minutes in a handful of games—I stopped hoping for a recovery and instead pushed myself to stay in a little longer each time no matter what. *If I don't sprint today*, I'd tell myself. Or, *if I don't try to pass more than a few yards*. But no matter how I tried to adjust, the muscle wouldn't hold.

A friend in the treatment room recommended a local doctor who said I couldn't do any more damage to the muscle and advised me to take twelve tablets of an over-the-counter painkiller called Aleve before each game. I started taking them before training sessions too.

The days got shorter. The air got colder. Out of the blue, my boyfriend dumped me. The season ended. Again I hadn't achieved any of the goals I had set for the team or myself. We finished with six wins, seven losses and two draws—nowhere near where we wanted to be. I gained about twenty pounds and blamed myself, feeling stupid once again like when I got sick in my freshman year. I should have known that if you aren't burning 3,000 calories a day on the field you shouldn't eat 3,000 calories a day anymore in the dining hall.

———

When I flew home for the December break from school, no one was allowed to visit Aaron except family. They weren't even letting Tom see him anymore.

My grandfather used his football connections to get me an appointment with the sports medicine specialist who treated the American football teams in the area, including Loyola, USC and UCLA. I was back on my home turf and was going to get the care I needed. I finally had an MRI of my quad.

When the doctor came to see me and my mom in the examination room, he slapped the image onto the lighted panel on the wall.

"Soccer's not the most important thing in your life, right?" he asked flippantly.

Without waiting for an answer, he continued, telling me that one of the four muscles in my quad—the deepest one, the vastus intermedius —was severed. He said it had snapped like a broken rubber band. That's how it felt—like it had disappeared from the middle of my thigh, leaving behind a painful hole. He told me there was an experimental surgical procedure to repair torn muscles like mine but that I wasn't a candidate for it. The surgery, he said, was for "elite athletes." I wanted to punch him in the face.

This was starting to feel familiar. Being laughed at for my big dreams. Being denied the family business. Being excluded from social clubs. Being denied a career-saving surgery. But I'm sure what he was thinking was that there was no professional women's soccer league. Women's soccer wasn't even in the Olympics yet. What could possibly necessitate him to open up my leg and attempt to manually reconstruct my quadricep? Nothing.

He didn't know that I wasn't even close to done. His casual dismissal of my career only made me more determined.

No one else suggested I quit. My parents didn't say: "Why don't you try something else?" Maybe they assumed I would get better. No one in my family had ever been hurt in that way, in a way that just never got better. My dad had had surgery on his shoulder in college. That's what you did—you had surgery and kept going.

Before we left the doctor's office, he suggested that steroids might help. I stopped in my tracks, wondering why he had waited until we were walking out the door to mention them. I opened my mouth to ask when and how. I was ready to take them, but my mom shut him down on the spot.

"Oh, no thank you," she said mid-stride and kept us both moving. "That's not for us."

All it took was a gentle push for her to keep me going out the door. I didn't have the energy to put up a fight. I didn't want to have an argument with my mom about using steroids. But if she had been open to it, I would have done it for sure.

———

Being dumped by my boyfriend before the end of the season had hurt. I had been totally blindsided. He wasn't sensitive. He told me straight up that he just wasn't attracted to me anymore. So humiliating. I wasn't in a good place so I couldn't even laugh about it. My sense of humor was MIA. I went through the post-break-up, total-waste-of-time guessing game about why he broke up with me. I didn't want to believe it but it did cross my mind that it was because of the weight I'd gained. Was it that simple and shallow? The seed of insecurity about my body replanted itself in my brain against my better judgment, and my strong self fought against my weak self for letting those toxic thoughts take root. I also began to realize how naive I was. I knew I had been letting him treat me poorly. But maybe I did need to wake up. Maybe he wasn't interested in me anymore because I was no longer the cute blonde freshman twin from Southern California starting on the women's soccer team. Maybe he never really liked me for me. Maybe he liked that image. I'd heard about people "using" other people. Could that be what had happened—that he'd used me? I was now an injured sophomore, thrown overboard. No trophy there. We were kids, both struggling, but I learned a lot.

Katie was also home over that school break and she was very thin at that time. I told myself she would know it was time to stop losing weight and that all she wanted was to get back to her normal weight. I wanted to get my old self back again too: confident, fast, strong and important to the team. I asked her what her trick for losing weight was. I told her what I was eating during the day, feeling pretty good about the fact that I'd started eating salads. She looked at me and said simply: "That's too much."

"Hmm. OK. Got it. Eat less," I said. The way she said it made me uneasy. I had to say something. "Kate, you know you shouldn't lose any more weight, right?"

"What?" she answered defensively. I suddenly felt on the spot. I almost said never mind. I didn't want to be at odds with her again like we had been throughout our younger years. I needed her in my life, but I'd admitted something to myself in my mind that I couldn't explain away. I was worried she didn't know when to stop.

I understood the reasons completely. The thinner the better, and the thinner the happier, are the general messages we are surrounded by in our society, and I was speaking to her from a position of being jealous that she had got down to her pre-Harvard weight. But I knew how she was about herself, super-critical about her looks and a relentless perfectionist in all things. Having just had my own insecurities about my boyfriend dumping me because of my weight, I worried that she had initially started losing weight to keep *her* boyfriend and now didn't know how to stop.

I said to Katie: "Remember the time mom said to us: 'You can never be too rich or too thin?'"

"Yeah," she replied, "she was joking."

"I know she was joking, but you do know that's not true, right?"

I told her I was having the same thoughts that my boyfriend lost interest in me because I'd gained weight—but the moment I realized that he was that type of person, I lost all respect for him, and my feelings for him faded on their own.

Handling and loving my body was a constant struggle, though. I began to notice dark hairs growing on my face and body where they hadn't been before. At first, they were easy to hide or tweeze. But the growth continued. I told my mom and she took me to another doctor a few days after the MRI on my quad. The doctor diagnosed me with polycystic ovary syndrome, which is caused by an imbalance of reproductive hormones. I had never had an ovarian cyst as far as I knew but the other symptoms I was having did fit. They included acne—which I'd struggled with since I was young—and excessive hair growth, which I was only just beginning to experience. And weight gain.

The doctor suggested a diuretic would slow the hair growth, but again my mom refused. I didn't put up a fight about that either. What would slowing the growth do, anyway? I needed a real solution but had nowhere to look for one. Outside that doctor's visit, my mom and I never spoke about the disorder again.

My mom coming in for a hug but then pinching my love handles didn't help my self-esteem at the time either. When I asked her to stop she said: "I'm sorry, I can't help it. My mom did more than that to me."

I swore I would never do that to my daughter should I be lucky enough to ever have one.

I went back to school after the new year and tried to hide what was happening. Trainers hadn't been able to help me and doctors didn't have the cures I needed either. It was all depressing. I didn't tell anyone about either of the diagnoses. Not even my teammates. Denial and shame are powerful forces.

I was still taking handfuls of pain medication even after the season was over, but I also found myself drinking more alcohol. It numbed the confusion and pain I was feeling and helped me forget about it all. I woke up a few times from a night out with no memory of how I got home.

I kept up my off-season commitments to the team and continued to reach out to the younger players the way the older girls had reached out to me when I was a freshman, asking them about their classes, their boyfriends, their families. Feeling like I had something to offer them— feeling needed—was something that always made me happy. But the things I was keeping secret started to affect my closest friendship.

Because Noonan was my teammate, best friend and roommate, she took the brunt of my moods and depression. One weekend, she and I joined a group of friends—mostly men from the junior varsity hockey team—and went to Yale for a party. I started drinking at the party along with everyone else but, like my worry about my sister and her eating, I lost sight of the limit. Something snapped. All the emotions I had been suppressing took over. I left the party by myself, frantic in my own head. My intention was to get out of the party and take a walk to calm down, but once I got outside I started to feel vulnerable walking around by myself in New Haven. I hated that feeling and hated myself for continuing to put myself in those situations. I got disoriented and didn't know which way I had come from. That's the last thing I remember.

My friends found me slumped outside the dorm where we were staying. I woke up to a boy touching my arm. It was our friend James trying to help bring me inside but I didn't see his face. My mind flashed back to the back seat of Romi's car and I started screaming and kicking to get him off me like I was finally defending myself with unrestrained power. Through my rage, I did eventually see the innocent faces of James and Noonan trying to help me. I knew I was being crazy but it was too late, and I was too tired and drunk to explain myself and make things right. I passed back out on the floor but woke up the next day inside in a bed. They had taken care of me.

The next time I saw James was in the training room.

"Hey, are you OK?" he asked.

I looked away, starting to cry. He waited a little while and then asked: "Do you want to go for a run with me tomorrow morning?"

Running was the one thing I could still do as long as I was careful to keep my stride short. I'd never been someone who loved running just to run, but the habit was growing on me. Running made me feel like I was making progress. It made all the muscles in my body feel that inimitable, wonderful soreness. He and I started running together in the mornings, meeting early before class, braving the cold to do intervals around the indoor track while the ROTC students (pronounced Rotsy, ROTC stands for Reserved Officer Training Corps and is the training program of the

United States armed forces on college campuses that recruits and trains future officers) performed their drills. I even enjoyed our arctic jogs along the frozen Charles River. He taught me how to pace myself and how to breathe properly. I realized that he believed I was going to get better. He was handsome and sweet and kinder to me than any boy had ever been before. It was impossible not to fall for him.

And then, one day, the unthinkable happened: he asked me if I shaved my face. The look on his face was one of disgust. I was so embarrassed and ashamed I didn't know what to do. I got up and got my things and ran out of the room, and then shut him out completely. The school year was almost over anyway. I thought I'd make a clean break and head home for the summer where I could concentrate on my training and focus on my junior season. And hide.

————

My mom had other plans. She was heading up the Los Angeles area volunteers for the 1994 FIFA Men's World Cup and had recruited everyone she could think of to help. Katie was dressing up as the mascot, Striker, posing for pictures with fans outside stadiums and World Cup-related events around the city. Tom was serving as a driver for FIFA officials and VIPs, navigating them around the city he had memorized while working delivery routes for our dad's business. My mom invited Noonan to live with us for the summer to work as a World Cup volunteer as well.

I was excited, of course. It was all a dream come true—the whole summer was going to be filled with soccer and friends coming and going. It felt like the United States had finally accepted soccer in a major way. And I loved Noonan so much and she had never failed me. But I failed her that summer. I was the worst hostess ever and an even worse friend. I was depressed and confused, desperate to figure out a way to play again, trying to figure out how things had fallen apart so badly. I was absorbed by my recovery and didn't have time for anything or anyone else. I gave up on my old way of playing and started relearning how to play without firing up that muscle. It wasn't that different to what had happened with my neurotic violinist boyfriend from freshman year—he had succeeded in teaching himself how to write with his left hand. I would teach myself to play soccer without my right quad.

As much as I loved the World Cup, I refused to take on any role with the tournament—except, of course, as a fan really just beginning to study the worldwide game. I got to see our US stars play, like the young Claudio Reyna, but I also became aware of a darker side of the game when Colombia's Andres Escobar scored an own goal against the US at the Rose Bowl on my twentieth birthday and he was executed when he got home to Medellín.

Noonan lived in our house with us but I only saw her a handful of times. While she was volunteering and meeting famous players from around the world, I spent the mornings at the gym, doing cardio and lifting weights, and then on empty fields near our house, juggling a ball, running laps, dribbling through cones, shuttling through suicides. I was trying to build up the muscles around the torn section of my quad to compensate as much as possible. I knew that to become an impact player again, I would have to become a much more technical player. I'd taken my speed for granted and now that it was gone, my mediocre technical skills were exposed. I stretched endlessly except for my right quad. If I pulled my foot behind me, I felt the tear. Every day I walked out onto the field, telling myself there *was* a way to play around it, but it was always there. A twinge of doom. I was carrying the end of my soccer career in my own body. My parents were busy with work and the World Cup. Katie was enjoying herself as Striker, and, when Tom wasn't working, his attention was on Aaron, whose condition seemed to have stabilized.

One day, I came back from my workout to find Noonan had packed her things and left.

"She flew out this morning," my mom said.

I hadn't even known she was leaving. She'd been all alone when she decided to leave. She packed herself up so far from home and got herself on a flight home. Got herself to the airport an hour away. Imagining her having to go through that all by herself—and that I'd been so removed

from what was going on in her life that I'd had no idea she was leaving
—I'd been a terrible friend to her. I'd disconnected from her. Had total
disregard for her feelings. Abandoned her. The depth of my self-absorption
hit me. The injury had been out of my control but the way I reacted to it
was all on me.

Not long after that, I received a letter from the housing department
at Harvard. As I opened it, I realized it wasn't going to be good news.
It said I had been placed in a single room that autumn. My roommates
had requested a three-person suite without me—I'd been kicked out of
my rooming group. I'd never heard of that happening before. My face
got hot and full of shame. No one else was home so I walked down the
hallway from my parents' kitchen into the back bedroom and sat down
on the big bed where I'd been sleeping that summer. I stared out the
window at the backyard where I'd spent so many hours falling deeper in
love with my game. My heart sank, and sank some more, until it hit the
bottom with a heavy thud.

I had no right to be surprised. I had isolated myself from them first. I
paused my self-flagellation for a moment, trying to convince myself that
at least I'd never abandoned the team—though I saw how warped that
was, as I'd believed what I was doing was *for* the team—but I'd messed
things up with my best friend and closest teammate and I would be lucky
if it didn't end up having a negative effect on the team.

There was still another problem. I recognized that I'd been isolating
myself, that I had hurt people, that I'd been selfish, but I didn't want
everything to change. I knew I needed to reevaluate the way I treated
people, but I genuinely believed that my training had been working—
that I was going to play again—and I wasn't ready to give up on that.

I had an image in my mind that I was drifting millions of
miles away from my old self, the girl who had control of her life.
It was time to take a good honest look at myself. The core of who
that girl was may have been happy on the soccer field, but she didn't
understand what being a good teammate or friend was. I imagined
the new person I wanted to be was at the center of a target—still

hard-working but a better person—but I had drifted so far away: insecurities, injury, lack of communication skills, a hormone disorder, unfortunate relationships with boys, so many things thrown in my path. I realized that what I needed was a reset.

Suddenly I felt like I had to have a paper and a pen. I stood up and rushed around the house, looking for something to draw on. I found a yellow pad and a black felt-tip marker and drew a small oval with two concentric rings around it. It was about an inch and a half in diameter. I was feeling an incredible sense of urgency but I didn't know why. Snatching my keys from the kitchen counter, I drove to a tattoo parlor. Within two hours, that symbol was tattooed on the back of my right shoulder.

And I didn't stop there. The next day, I had Romi drive me to a Supercuts in a local shopping center. She still had the little white Volkswagen convertible. Sitting in the front passenger seat, I imagined a struggle going on behind me. When we walked into the salon, I sat down in one of the chairs and asked the stylist to shave my head. The stylist resisted, taking a step back from me and pulling the salon robe she was holding in toward her body instead of handing it to me to put on. Romi was sitting in the next chair, squeezing her knees tight into her chest with her arms and grimacing. I was hurt. I felt like I was empowering myself. I thought Romi would feel empowered with me. Some of the wind was knocked out of my sails, but I wasn't going to be deterred.

As the stylist started shaving my head, each pass of the buzzer made me feel closer to some urgent destination. After a few minutes, she turned the buzzer off. I felt the soft, prickly buzz with my hands. Where my hair had been heavy, now my scalp felt free.

Afterwards, I made Romi stop at the drug store for hair dye, and when I got home I dyed the remaining buzz cut blue.

That night, I had no choice but to reveal my new look to my father, who was sitting in his usual after-work chair with a stack of work and a bottle of beer. I was on an adrenaline high and had a huge smile on my face even though inside I was terrified of his reaction. I took off the stretchy beanie I was wearing and said: "Ta da!"

He didn't move. His face grew angry. Angrier than I'd ever seen it. But he never made a move like he was going to get out of his chair.

"Susan," he said through gritted teeth, "I don't like it, and I don't even think it's *funny*."

His tone was biting especially toward the end. His outrage blew through me like a mushroom cloud, but after it passed I was still standing. I had known the reveal wasn't going to go well. I wasn't trying to be funny, and I knew he would hate it. But I also knew there was no good way to show him. No right time. No buttering him up for this one.

The tattoo marks that moment in my life. When I left for college, my father had told me to take the time to appreciate special moments and, despite my immaturity, I was self-aware enough to know that painful moments can be special too. I wanted to always remember the day I'd started over, how down I had got, how low I had sunk, how untethered I had become. I felt—for the first time—that I had taken the first twenty years of my life for granted: the opportunities I'd had on the field, my health, my talent, my body, the love and support (however complicated) of my family and my friendships. I believed that if I put a permanent mark on myself, I wouldn't let that happen again—or at least I would be less likely to.

This was a new me. And only me; it would be decades before anyone would mistake me for my sister again. The new me would aim to be more self-aware and less self-absorbed. Would intend to be a better person. And realize I'd taken myself too seriously.

———

When I got back to Harvard in the autumn of my junior year I was excited about preseason but sad that things had deteriorated so badly with Noonan. I had felt good about my fresh start, but after the adrenaline wore off I saw a long road ahead, and it was sad to move into my single room. Shortly after I returned to campus, our coach Tim came up to me in the treatment room. My new haircut and living situation hadn't gone unnoticed.

"I've made you an appointment with someone at the counseling center," he said. He told me where to go and when. And, because he didn't give me a choice in the matter, I went. It felt so good to have someone guide me toward a new kind of help. It was a pivotal moment.

At my first appointment at the counseling center, I was surprised. The counselor was not what I expected a Harvard staff member to look like. I guess I expected someone older and more polished. More judgy. The woman who greeted me looked more like a flower child from the Sixties—like a young Stevie Nicks. After some small talk, she waited for me to start from the beginning. I had no idea where to begin. In my mind, I retraced the previous couple of years. Suddenly overwhelmed, I started to sob uncontrollably. I didn't get another word out that first session. She handed me a box of tissues and we just sat there while I cried.

At the end of the hour, she told me to come back the next day at the same time. I saw her twice a week for the rest of my time at Harvard. I started with the worst shame: how I ruined my friendship with Noonan, how selfish I'd been, how depressed. I told her about my injury. That I lost my happiness when I lost my leg. I admitted I believed the people who told me that I'd got in to Harvard as an athlete and wasn't considered a real Harvard student. I told her about my first boyfriend who dumped me because I wouldn't have sex with him, the assault in the back seat of Romi's car, the violinist boyfriend who dumped me, the polycystic ovary syndrome. On we went, session after session, tracing certain struggles, like with my sister, back to childhood. I told her I was keeping an eye on my sister's weight. She recommended a specialist that my sister started to go to for professional care to make sure there was nothing to be concerned about. She suggested something called electrolysis as a permanent solution to the hair growth, which turned out to be nothing short of medieval torture and prohibitively expensive, but did work. I doubled down on my studies, enrolling in organic chemistry as an elective to prove to myself that I could handle any class at Harvard, earning my highest grade ever. I looked forward to seeing her every time. Over the weeks and months, things started to get brighter.

On the field, there were improvements too. Noonan and I had lost our special connection because I'd pulled so far away from her, but we worked well together on the field as we always had. Just as when my sister and I were not getting along when we were younger, we always worked together on the field no matter what. We left the other stuff off the field. I was back playing in the middle along with a freshman named Emily Stauffer —the talented sister of Matt Stauffer, the boy who had struck me with his honest player assessments at the Stanford camp in high school. With Tim's guidance, I succeeded in adjusting my style of play, retreating to a more defensive role and only making short passes. I was more conservative in my mindset, forgoing the reckless abandon I'd played with for so long in the hope of pleasing my father. To help my team, I had to play smarter not tougher. I was finally starting to adapt.

Tim had put together a great line-up that season. In addition to Stauffy, there were six other freshmen who immediately started making contributions to the team. One in particular stood out for me. Her name was Lindsay Minkus but everyone called her Mink (and occasionally Cockroach, after a pathetic battle with a horde of the species in one of our preseason dorm rooms). She was loud and always laughing. None of the freshman initiations bothered her in the least. When her class showed up for our first bus trip—as directed by the senior players—she stood and belted out Whitney Houston's "I Will Always Love You" when it was her turn to stand at the front. She was happy to stay up there, sharing stories about herself or anyone else, until we made her sit down so we could hear from another freshman.

Mink later told me she had me pegged by the end of our first day of preseason. We were sitting in a circle, listening to Tim talk about upcoming fitness tests, and she was going around the circle studying each of her new teammates. When she got to me, she took a minute. She observed I was wearing a pair of old overalls and a concert t-shirt, my hair a very short outgrown buzz cut, now blue just at the tips. Mink first assumed I was the cool twin—some kind of badass. But as she continued to watch me, I discovered something was in my pocket. She saw me pull the thing out of my pocket, recognize it and quickly shove it back in with a reddening face.

We had all had our preseason physicals that morning. I had taken a handful of condoms from a large bowl on the counter of the health services office on my way out. I'd thought they were sweets and my hand was already deep in the bowl when I realized what they actually were. Instead of just retreating and letting go of them—I really had no use for them at the time—I decided to take them. I put them in my pocket, feeling like quite the bold twenty-year-old woman that I was. But I had forgotten about them. When I blushed and tried to tuck the condoms away without anyone seeing, Mink said she knew: I wasn't so tough.

Mink made me her friend—and it was good timing. I was on my way to becoming a more mindful, healthier person so, unlike with other friendships I'd had, I didn't take her for granted even for a second. We studied together, sat next to each other on road trips, went to concerts, explored the city. As good as Mink was at soccer, it turned out that soccer was actually her third-best sport after tennis and ice hockey; some girls grew up with more opportunities than girls where I was from. She introduced me to Thai food, sushi and Indian food. Mink immediately saw me for who I really was, and understood things about me that it had taken me years to figure out.

When she asked me about my tattoo, for instance, I struggled to put into words my feelings about drifting away from my core. She understood immediately.

"It's like your orbits," she said.

"Yes. Yes," I said, wondering how she could have come up with that so quickly. And that's how I've thought about it ever since.

When her mom and sister met me a month later, they both pulled her aside separately and asked: "Are you *sure* she's your closest friend?"

And she replied both times: "Absolutely."

———

Things were looking up. And our team was *good*. After drawing with

Columbia in our first Ivy League match of the season (a game we should have won), we started to win. In our second conference contest, we beat Yale by two goals at home even with Stauffy having to play the second half of the game with a soft cast on her left forearm after suffering a hairline fracture. The training staff took her inside and we all thought she was out, but a few minutes later she came running back out onto the field with a giant soft cast, ready to get back in the game. I still have no idea how she convinced them to let her get back out there but I've loved her for it ever since. She is the toughest little thing.

That night starting in the Radcliffe Quad, we celebrated Harvard style: we stood in double-line formation the way we did for pre-match warm-ups, faced the nearest American flag and sang the "Star Spangled Banner" at the top of our lungs—a long, completely out-of-tune primal scream. Then we stripped out of our clothes, leaving everything in a massive pile with one of the freshmen and a pair of recruits, and ran all the way into Harvard Square and down Massachusetts Avenue, singing: "Olé, Olé, Olé, Oléééé... Harvarrrrrd... Harvarrrrrrd..." Noonan was running in her red cowboy boots. At one point, we crossed paths with a group in formal white-tie attire exiting the Hasty Pudding building.

"Sorry!" I yelled, giggling uncontrollably when I smashed into the back of a very tall gentleman with a top hat and cane.

The police who were directing the traffic outside the Hasty Pudding called an audible, like when the quarterback in an American football game reads the situation and shouts out a last-second change in the play after the huddle, and decided to provide us with an escort. Someone ran into the Grille and announced that the women's soccer team was streaking through Harvard Square, and two of our teammates who we had excused from the festivities to attend dates with guys at the Grille jumped up and ran to meet us, calling an abrupt end to their dates. Eventually we ran back through the arches of Kirkland House, where a bunch of us were living, sprinting up the stairs to Noonan's room, waving to Bob the security guard—making his night, I'm sure—as we passed.

After Yale, we beat Princeton. Then we faced nationally ranked

Dartmouth at home. Going into the ninetieth minute, we were drawing 1-1. With just seconds to go, Noonan blasted a ball into the back of the net. Our fans—including the men's team—rushed onto the field to celebrate with us. The win was a huge upset and kept us in the running for the Ivy League title.

Brown was our final opponent, and they were one point ahead of us in the Ivy League standings because of our draw with Columbia earlier in the season. We had to win to take the title; Brown only had to draw. Winning the Ivy League had been my highest priority since the instant I landed at Harvard, and for my soccer career it was the closest I would ever get to a gold medal. I wanted that title. I had to have it. I had become *obsessed*. My parents made the long flight out from Los Angeles to Boston for the big game.

Toward the end of the game, we were leading 3-1. We could smell the title, and taste it. But Brown wasn't finished. With just a few minutes to go, they scored on a quick, well-executed counterattack. They were now only one goal down. We pushed back, but I could feel the tide of the game turning. Not long after they scored, they won a corner. The cross came in and a Brown player headed the ball toward me. I panicked. *Then* I jumped to defend the shot. It was too late. The ball was over my head. By the time I turned it was already bouncing off the back of the net behind me.

Time ran out. The whistle blew. Brown went crazy. I squatted down, putting my hands on the cold grass and, eventually, over my face. We had come up short by seconds and inches. The worst part was that we had let down our seniors; this was their last chance at an Ivy Championship.

My teammates consoled me. My dad came to find me on the field, still in that same spot, processing the loss and my role in it. He made me stand up, put his arms around me, and slowly walked us across the road toward the dressing room.

Along the way, we ran into my friend Matty who was hosting his normal tailgate party outside the football stadium. Ever since our freshman year, whenever our games aligned with the football games, he rallied his crew to walk across the street to come and harass and rattle our opponents.

He gave me a bear hug and wiped away my tears with his t-shirt. After I introduced him to my dad, he offered us both a beer. It was odd. Instead of mourning the season, beating myself up over my failure to stop the header, I was bonding with my dad over ice-cold beer from a keg. I felt guilty, worried it was too soon to be enjoying myself. By the time I got to the dressing room, I was already dreaming about getting our revenge.

But we had another game to play before that. For the first time in ten years, our team was honored to be selected to play in the National Collegiate Athletics Association (the NCAA runs the national championship tournaments for college sports in the United States) post-season tournament and would have a chance to play for the national championship. I started to hear people say we'd made it to "the Big Dance." They congratulated us. Patted us on the back. It felt like we'd made it to the inside of the rainbow, a place reserved for only the elite players. When the draw was announced, we found out we would face the University of Massachusetts. On the day of the game, Ohiri Field was decked out in NCAA regalia. People actually had to pay to watch us play for the first time. It felt like the big time.

Unfortunately, we lost big time: 0-3, with Brianna Scurry, the future Women's National Team goalie and World Cup Champion, keeping a clean sheet and ending our season.

Our consolation prize was watching the Harvard men play in Providence in their first-round NCAA tournament game. To show our school spirit, we each painted letters on our stomach to spell "GO HARVARD!" But once we were assembled in the top row, freezing in just our sports bras, we were lined up backwards and spelled "!DRAVRAHOG" instead. From then on, we stuck with "Dravrahog!" as our rallying cry.

A couple of weeks later, we gathered for a team meeting in our dressing room and Noonan and I were voted cocaptains for the upcoming season. We shared a look. Strained friendship aside, we had a common purpose and passion. We were determined to take the Ivy League title in our senior year. I was proud to be chosen as a leader alongside her, and I was building up the courage to apologize to her. I may not have been able to contribute to the team with goals and assists as I'd hoped to, but the opportunity to have these remarkable women as my teammates and follow in the footsteps of the great leaders of the team—captains included—was the honor of a lifetime.

That night, Katie told me she was quitting the team. She was ready to be done with soccer. She said it was because of her knee—she had a recurring knee injury that she struggled with—but I worried she had made the decision at least in part because she wasn't voted captain. So many times we'd experienced this; if one of us got something it meant the other was left out. We weren't both happy at the same time very often. Our closeness went in phases and her quitting soccer was the beginning of another emotional separation between us.

My sister and I looked less like identical twins than ever because of my now-shaggy short hairstyle, but my need to be more different wasn't yet exhausted. My sister had never strayed from her classy, traditional, feminine style, while I'd appropriated the baggy jeans and flannel shirts that was the "grunge" style of the time, but one night I tried out a new style. I picked khaki trousers, a white dress shirt and a loosely knotted men's tie. I figured out how to knot the tie in the mirror in my single room, smoothing the shirt down under the waist of my trousers. Looking at myself in the mirror, I liked the look with my laidback, disheveled hairstyle. I wanted to wear what made me feel good in the moment, I didn't want to care if people labelled them girl clothes or boy clothes. I felt sexy and powerful. Defiant.

I left my room, went out the front door of my building and walked to the library. After sitting there for a while, unable to study, I went home and changed my clothes. Those clothes weren't me. I felt conspicuous, too dressed up. That's not who I was. I was still searching. But I felt brave for trying.

———

After the season finished, I had a "Holy shit!" moment: I realized I had enough credits to take a semester off from school and still graduate on time.

Our team had been so close to winning an Ivy League Championship that we had proven that it was possible. Noonan and I only had one season left to win it all. As isolating as it had been, my training the summer before had worked: I had relearned how to play with my injury, earned a starting central midfield position, and we had almost won the title. I planned to train again like that, but also to avoid the winter in Boston. I was going to take the spring semester off.

I spoke to my parents, who agreed. They didn't know what was going on with me but they were sympathetic—plus they were off the hook for a semester's tuition costs and I would still be graduating on time. Tim was supportive, as he had been all along. My one regret was not being there to run the spring captain's training sessions, but I knew Noonan was there to take care of them.

I spent Christmas with my family in the house I grew up in, and then moved into a condo my parents had recently bought in Newport Beach, overlooking Newport Bay and four blocks from the beach. It was an unreal set-up. It was like a blip in time that I wasn't sure how I'd made happen. I took a job at an ice cream shop and worked there every afternoon, scooping cones and cups for happy kids on their way to or from the beach. In the mornings, I went back to my routine: long hours at the gym running on the treadmill, lifting weights and stretching, and then ball skills at a local field. After I finished my workout, my reward was to juggle the ball, which was my favorite part of my day.

I had never been a great ball juggler—I could knock out twenty or so keepie-uppies on my feet and thighs—but that spring, I spent mornings in the sun in my sports bra and shorts at the local park, feeling free and happy, working on my freestyle, letting the ball roll over my shoulders, chest and arms. Eventually I could catch the ball on the back of my neck or my chest and drop it back down to the instep of my feet without thinking about it. I worked on every trick I had ever seen—getting some, tripping over others, and every day getting just a little bit better at each one.

One day, as I finished my workout, a guy who had been running at the other end of the field came up and started talking to me. He said he was on leave from the Marines. After chatting for a bit, he asked me if I'd like to go to a movie, and I said yes. Unfortunately it was the most awkward date of my life. It didn't matter that he was nice and respectful—and he was both of those things. I couldn't relax and be myself.

All he wants is sex, I kept thinking to myself. *All he wants is sex.*

It wasn't fair to think that. I knew that, but I couldn't help it. I couldn't connect with him at all. *What's the point?* I thought.

I wanted to be by myself, but at the same time I was lonely. I started driving over to my brother Tony's house in the Belmont Shore neighborhood of Long Beach that was full of cute little bungalows. He had got married the previous fall, and I loved spending time with him and his wife. They seemed like they were creating the perfect little family.

Tony and I were spending a lot of time together at the weekends, driving around the back roads of Los Angeles and through the canyons of Hollywood. We had become very close, and I had decided to open up to him about something I'd been thinking about for a long time.

I'd recently had conversations with different groups of friends where the topic of sexuality had come up. If the question about sexuality came to me my answer had become: "I think everyone is bisexual." That was my truth. That's what felt honest to me, and Tom always taught me to be honest no matter what. He was never afraid to follow his own moral compass, regardless of what he predicted other people's reactions would be. I know people were thinking: *Um no, not everyone is bisexual. I'm not bisexual, but clearly* you *are.* I knew most people were only interested in traditional relationships and were not going to agree with me. But I felt attracted to both boys and girls and I honestly felt like most people might be confining themselves to traditional sexuality roles because that's what we were taught. Tom always stuck up for his friends and had a zero-tolerance policy for injustices like racism and homophobia so, to me, this was my way of following his example and also being true to myself.

Tony pulled his car into the driveway of our parents' house for dinner and neither of us got out of the car. *Just say it*, I told myself. Telling my big brother so directly like this was very different to challenging a bunch of college friends with a controversial statement.

"I have to tell you something," I said. "I think I'm bisexual."

I let out the breath I'd been holding and waited for him to say something. Instead, he burst out laughing.

"That's an odd response," I said, having no idea why what I had told him was funny, and regretting saying it.

"I'm sorry," he said. "I know it's not funny. It's just so weird. I was about to tell you the same thing."

A year later Tony was divorced. A couple of years after that he met his current partner, Gary, and they've been together ever since. He must have heard all those jokes like the ones I'd heard too. I thought about how we had all assumed that we knew who Tony was, and I started to see how hard he'd tried to assume that role. Expressing he was bisexual was a big step toward coming out for him. Expressing I was bisexual was a big step toward self-awareness for me.

———

At some point, I called Kim, my best friend from our ODP team. We had talked sporadically after going away to college (she played at a small school in northern California). Sometimes I called her dorm phone or she called mine, and we wrote a few letters back and forth. Any time we spoke, it was as if we had never got off our shared bus seat during that first ODP road trip together so long ago. Now she was home on a school break to visit her dad who lived not too far from my parents' condo. I hadn't seen her since high school, but when I saw her again it was like no time had passed. When I was with her, I didn't worry about anything. I was happy.

My schedule changed once we connected. I pushed my morning workouts back because Kim got up early, drove down in her red Bronco and took me surfing. Or rather, she surfed and I watched. She tried to drag me in but I refused. I hadn't surfed since high school, and was never very good at it. Besides, I had come home to California to be warm not cold; going into the ocean seemed no different to going back into winter. Also I was nervous about damaging my quad and how I would manage, single-legged, in the big waves so far from the shore. I was perfectly content to watch Kim from the beach, where I sat bundled up in a hoodie and blankets. When she was done surfing, we would sit together on the lifeguard station, eating enormous breakfast burritos.

I never felt more like myself than I did when I was with Kim, and that had started all the way back when we were on the ODP team together, bonding during those long bus rides and in shared hotel rooms. I opened up to her about the way I had treated Noonan the summer before.

"You should just talk to her. She'll understand," she said, and then added: "And, you know, we all have something about ourselves like that... something that we're hard on ourselves about."

I knew she was right.

I quit my job at the ice cream shop so we could hang out together in the afternoons, and sometimes she slept over at my parents' condo with me. One night, after a few beers, she convinced me that I had to get back in the water. We stormed into a surf shop across the street, bought the thickest wet suit they had in stock and, after squeezing ourselves into our gear in the apartment, ran down the street to the docks, jumping into the dark water off an empty boat slip.

It should have been scary, but nothing felt frightening when Kim was around—not my anxiety about guys, not my struggles with my confidence in school, and certainly not a little night swimming. At the bottom of my descent into the dark water of the bay, I opened my eyes and looked up toward the surface. The silence was eerie. I wasn't cold at all. In fact, I was comfortable. The lights on the dock illuminated small circles in the water above me in murky glowing green spots but, other than that, everything was pitch black and quiet. In no rush, I started to swim my way back up. Then, something hit me in the face and bounced off my arm and then my leg. I squinted, trying hard to make out the form of whatever it was. Something made me shiver and the next thing I knew I was completely flipping out and scrambling out of the water onto the wet dock. Kim was already out and laughing hysterically at my panicky exit. We had jumped into a swarm of jellyfish.

When it was time for Kim to go back to school I wasn't ready to say goodbye.

"Why don't you come with me?" she asked.

I couldn't think of a single reason to say no.

On the drive north, we stopped at her boyfriend Ernie's house in Santa Cruz, across from a stretch of the coast called Pleasure Point where the waves broke slowly and easily. Kim had given me a pep talk about getting in the water for the length of the drive.

"Today is your day to get back on the board," she said.

It was a perfect afternoon. The sky was clear and blue, I had my heavy wetsuit, and the sun was blazing hot, so she knew I couldn't give her my usual excuse about the cold water. We suited up in our gear and climbed down the boulders to a little mini-beach of packed, wet sand. Ernie met us at the bottom, having carried down the rocks a canoe-like board that would provide more stability for me. My heart was pounding so hard I could hardly hear. Kim was a few steps in front of me as we waded into the water, but her voice seemed far away.

I followed her actions as closely as possible. The channel was calm, just like she had promised, and I was happy to be paddling behind her. But I was also *terrified*. After a few minutes, I was relieved to see her sit up on her board. I did the same.

Once I was out in the water, I realized I was shivering. I knew I shouldn't be cold. The sun was hot and my wetsuit was really too heavy for the conditions. I told myself to stop it, but it was more than just a shiver I was feeling. I was shaking uncontrollably. I tried to calm myself down but I couldn't and it was making it impossible to stay steady on the board. I wanted to be sitting out there peacefully, enjoying the day, the weather, the view.

I realized that it wasn't the cold that was making me shake. It was fear. I was afraid. I was always terrible at surfing but it had been fun anyway. But now it had been years, and if my leg couldn't handle the strain, I wasn't ready to be disappointed again. My worry was justified;

simply straddling the massive board was stretching my quad to the point of pain. But I didn't want to fail again.

I kept coming back to Kim's belief in me. She was so certain in me, exactly as she'd always been as a teammate. Now I just needed my body to be with me, and I needed to be proud of myself for trying.

The swells were like huge, gentle giants. This was the stuff I missed about California when I was at school: the crazy-blue sky, the hot sunshine, the amazing Pacific Coast, Kim, myself. The shaking subsided and I had a peaceful moment on the board. The feeling then settled inward and I sensed a new confidence rising in me about life in general again.

A wave approached. Kim told me to follow her, and I did, carefully moving my right leg back to lie on the board. I started to paddle, digging my hands into the cold water to start moving forward. Eventually my board started to drop slowly into the wave behind Kim's. I knew I had to be patient. After a while, Kim popped up in front of me, signaling it was time for me to do the same. I pushed hard off the board with my arms and got my left foot almost to the proper position in the front, but my right leg hadn't popped up. My right knee was still down on the board behind me in an awkward way. The muscles and tendons in my right thigh stretched out uncomfortably.

Feeling like I wasn't going to be able to lift my right leg, I considered bailing but decided to give it one big try. I took a deep breath and shifted my weight to my left leg. Concentrating on balancing on that left leg, I leaned as far forward as I could and my right leg rose off the board. I didn't have great control of that right leg so I turned my body and hoped my right foot would find the board. It all had to come together in just the right way in that split second. And it did. I let out the breath I'd been holding.

Kim was right; the waves at that break were forgiving. The swell I was on held that longboard even and steady for an eternity, allowing me to maneuver myself clumsily. Now standing on the board, the California coast was blindingly bright and sparkly in front of me. I rode that wave all the way to shore, where Kim and Ernie were hooting and clapping. Once I made it to shallow water, I stretched out my arms above my head and let myself fall sideways into the cold ocean. All I'd been seeing was what I couldn't do.

A few days later when we arrived in San Francisco, where Kim was going to school, I reached out to a friend in the area named Antonio Rossmann, who asked me to join him on a 31-mile training run. He was a long-time referee who was also an ultra-marathoner. When he asked me, I laughed on the phone: "You're crazy!"

At that point in my life, I'd never run more than a few miles in a single stretch. But after we talked, I couldn't get the idea out of my head. He said he knew I could do it. I realized that, again, I was the one holding myself back. All I had to do was believe I could do it too. I had to stop feeling sorry for myself. My body had one new limitation—just one—and I had to stop putting other false limitations on my body. I cut off my big heavy mental chains and let them drop to the ground with an earth-shaking *thud*.

"I'm in," I said when I called him back.

"Great!" he cried. "Bring petroleum jelly."

I knew what the lube was for, and the thought kicked up a whole batch of butterflies in my stomach: this was going to be painful. That Saturday, I met him at his house, and he taught me how to grease up my inner thighs and underarms with the petroleum jelly to minimize chafing. And off we went.

We ran on the dirt trails over the Berkeley Hills behind UC Berkeley to a town called Lafayette, where we stopped to use the toilet and eat an energy bar. Then we continued on through some of the prettiest scenery in California: rolling hills with oak trees, dry pastures, small ponds, creeks, horses, cows, and at one point a formidable-looking bull that we scooted cautiously around. When things got tough, I sang James Brown's "I Feel Good" over and over to myself. It worked. I *did* feel good. The hardest part was the last mile, all steep downhills. Without a full right quad, that stretch took a toll on the surrounding muscles.

Back at Kim's dorm, I took a shower, drank a huge bottle of water and threw myself on the bottom bunk I was borrowing. I woke up just about twenty-four hours later, dizzy and with the stiffest, sorest legs I'd ever had in my life. But also proud.

I spent a few days with Kim, recovering, and then, once I could walk normally again, hitched a ride with my parents as they were passing through on their way home from visiting some college friends.

As we were driving, my parents got a frantic call from my sister. There had been a fire in her dorm room. No one had been seriously injured, but the fire and then the water from the sprinkler system had destroyed most of her belongings. And the experience had been terrifying.

My mom didn't hesitate. She grabbed a few things, had us drop her at the nearest airport and flew immediately to be with Katie. I wanted to do the same but didn't feel comfortable asking my parents to pay for an extra ticket since I was the one who had chosen to take the semester off. If I hadn't done that, I would have been with Katie to begin with.

The more I thought about Katie, the more I thought about my teammates, and I knew I needed to be back with all of them. I needed to get back where I belonged and savor every moment I had left with the team and not just the results we produced. It was a good feeling. But I had made a different choice just a few months before—to leave them on their own and return home for the spring semester. Maybe I would lose my position on the team. Maybe they would choose someone else as captain in my absence. I knew if that happened I would only have myself to blame.

Yet, when I got back to Newport Beach, Mink called. She said she had been trying to reach me for days—she, Stauffy and two of our other teammates were coming to visit me for their spring break. They had already bought their tickets.

"We want to see our captain," she said.

Her words went straight to my heart. I was so happy I started to cry in a spontaneous burst of emotion. I felt so fortunate for her friendship and for the love of my teammates.

It turned out that those sneaky girls did have one ulterior motive: they wanted me to take them skydiving.

I deserved this because I had bragged about the time I jumped out of a plane with Romi to celebrate her eighteenth birthday. (Actually, the relief I felt when my parachute opened as I fell from the sky the first time was just like the feeling I experienced when Mink called me to say they were coming to visit: a spontaneous burst of wet, happy sobs; two *major* it's-all-going-to-be-OK moments.) They didn't know I had no desire to go skydiving again—in fact, I was *fucking terrified* of doing it again—but I couldn't let my teammates down. When the day arrived, I drove us all to the airfield and, just like Romi and I had done, we skipped the quicker tandem-dive option and spent several hours in training for free dives.

Jumping out of the plane turned out to be easier the second time around. I was still scared but this time I was less worried about death and more worried about my teammates. I was responsible for them, and I knew Tim and everyone's parents would *murder* me if I took out half our starting line-up in one reckless move over spring break. But everything went fine. We all landed safely on the ground, and we rushed together in a big hug just like we did on the field after a goal, panting and laughing and full of pride and sweat and sweet, sweet relief.

The rest of the week went by in a happy blur. We ran on the beach in the mornings, with Stauffy leading us in visualizations of winning the Ivy League Championship. She said if she could see it she could make it happen, so we all eagerly joined in. We laid in the warm sun every afternoon. I felt happy and loved and I valued my teammates' friendship for what it was: the most special gift in my life.

———

My mom had a big surprise for me that summer: a trip for the two of us to watch the 1995 FIFA Women's World Cup in Sweden. I couldn't believe it, and not just because I would get to see my idols playing in person and on the world stage for the first time. My mom never traveled without my father; she didn't make big financial decisions like spending money on a trip out of the country without my father; she didn't do very much without my father. And he never did anything without her. The question of what he would eat when she wasn't around was a legitimate concern. But maybe her worry for him was overtaken by her worry about me.

Apart from my teammates' visit and my time with Kim, I was like a hermit living by myself in Newport Beach. My mom didn't know—because we didn't talk—that I was more determined than ever to do well, for myself and for my team. Maybe she was worried I was going to drop out of school like my older brother had for a time. However she made it happen, she and I got on a plane to Sweden and spent three weeks traveling around the country with just our backpacks.

I woke up early every morning to work out before breakfast and often went to bed before her to make sure I got enough sleep. But the rest of the time, we were together. With so much time on our own, I started to hear her stories for the first time. I heard about what it was like for her growing up on a dirt road in rural Connecticut with no dad. How her mom had worked nights at a local hospital as a nurse and got home just in time to get her three kids on the bus for school. How she'd never even bought a box of tampons, never mind used one, before the day she bought them for me. How her high school had had only one sport for girls, half-court basketball, which she'd loved. How she'd studied for the SAT, dreaming of going to college far away in the West, where she thought she would be free but instead found a dress code for female students on campus at Stanford (they weren't allowed to leave their dorms without a skirt on) and a curfew, also just for women. About the limited options in the workplace for women when she graduated. About how she had found a job working for the phone company and then spent a year in the Peace Corps in Colombia before quitting to raise a family. She said my dad saved her. She'd missed him terribly when she was away in Colombia and she got very sick; he'd traveled there to get her, nurse her back to health and bring her home. They were married a year later—my dad's family drove across the country so they could get married in my mom's home town in rural western Connecticut with her family. The pictures of the happy young couple are very sweet. She also told me more about her mother: not only had her mother supported them by working nights as a nurse, but she had been limited to being a nurse while everyone in the rural hospital knew she should have been allowed to become a doctor.

As my mother's stories continued I started to feel so sad. I hadn't really seen her or my grandmothers before. I was sad that I hadn't valued their stories the way I'd valued my father's and grandfather's stories. I'd felt some of those same feelings, denied as a women. I began to feel like I was starting to understand my mother and her mother and all of our mothers. Or to at least appreciate that I needed to know so much more about what they had gone through.

By the end of the trip, we were really opening up to each other. We talked about my tattoo, and she said she wished it were "prettier" but she listened intently when I told her what it meant to me, how it had become kind of like a target for who I wanted to be. It felt good to share with her where I really was in life. We talked about Katie. We both admired her innate ambition and dedication to her education and felt bad that she sometimes wasn't taken seriously because she was too pretty. We laughed because we agreed she really was an introverted geek who didn't want the incessant attention she got from boys.

"We were always so worried about the two of you becoming individuals," my mom said. "Maybe we should have just left you alone. Let your paths happen naturally." I had always thought she wanted us to be different, but she was really just trying to give us permission to be ourselves.

Meanwhile, I couldn't believe what I saw at the Women's World Cup. Sweden was a hotbed for women's soccer. Unlike the United States, it had a women's professional league, so the stadiums and fan base were already in place. There were crowded venues to watch the games on screens, and people were partying in the streets. The stadiums were perfectly sized; we were able to get an up-close view of all the players. Mary Harvey was there again, plus Kristine Lilly, Michelle Akers, Mia Hamm. Also girls I had played against, including Jen Lalor, Foudy and MacMillan. I was in awe of them. All the teams from all over the world.

We watched as the US women lost a heartbreaker in the semi-final to Norway. But my mom—who talks to anyone and everyone and knew many of the tournament administrators from her volunteer work the year before—found out the team was hosting a get-together for friends and family (we might have been the only American fans at the tournament who weren't friends or family) and scored an invite to the post-game party. I was too scared to go. I don't know why it was so scary to go and meet my idols. I was impressed with my mom's attitude—she wasn't afraid at all. She tried to coax me into going with her but I just couldn't.

When my mom got back, she said she had met everyone and had even talked to Foudy about their Stanford connection. That was a tough lesson about missed opportunities and not being such a wimp.

———

My senior season finally arrived. Noonan and I had still not discussed what happened to our friendship the summer before. But we didn't let that stop us from working together on the first order of business and one of the most coveted privileges of being captain: the pre-game playlist for the loud speaker on Ohiri Field.

We were in the Kirkland House dining hall, each with our lists of favorite pump-up songs. The first one on her list was Gloria Gaynor's "I Will Survive" so we started going through the tune and the lyrics. She knew it better than I did and as she sang through each line I hummed along. Right from the first two lines, that special thing started to happen when a song grows into your heart because it speaks to you.

Listening along, I related to the words. I *had* been very afraid and I *had* spent many nights feeling like I'd been wronged. But in the midst of listening, I realized I'd spent *too many* days and weeks feeling that way… like I'd been wronged. How wronged had I been *really* when my life was like this? I was sitting in a Harvard dining hall with my cocaptain, picking pump-up music in preparation for the most exciting twelve weeks —win or lose—of my life. I'd allowed myself to become absorbed by the bad things that had happened to me and I had failed to appreciate the blessings around me. But that was over. That was done. I wanted to be better than that.

Noonan was singing the last lines of the song in the dining hall with no inhibitions. I wasn't the only one chuckling and everyone in the dining hall applauded her performance when she finished. The song was perfect. Noonan was so right. The song was about recognizing a bad relationship and kicking it out the door. For our team it was about taking the painful loss at the end of last season and carrying on. It was about standing up on your own two feet, dropping the self-pity, and letting tough times make you stronger.

"It's so perfect, Noonan. It's awesome," I said.

I hadn't been grateful. For me, that's really what it boiled down to. Sitting there with Noonan, so grateful to be hanging out with her again, I became tearful.

"I'm so sorry about last summer and how awful I was to you. It had nothing to do with you. I was depressed and wanted my leg back but I... no, no 'buts'... I was immature and scared and was shutting everyone out. I'm so sorry."

She put her arms around me and said: "Aww, don't cry. You're going to make me cry. It's OK. I just didn't understand it. I had no idea what was going on. You seemed normal just that you were choosing to live a totally separate life from me all of a sudden. I missed you. It was so confusing. It really did hurt. You left me all alone."

"I know. I'm so sorry. I was lost. Totally lost. But I know now. I know what I did. I was stuck. I thought I had to do everything on my own. I'm working on it," I said.

Through my tears my mind went back to seventh-grade math class. When it wasn't easy, I didn't put in work. Friendships with teammates were easy when I was healthy, when there was tons to be happy about and tons of prearranged time together to bond, but as soon as something got tough and I had to actually work to be a friend, I failed to do that.

She hugged me for a long time. Wiping away our tears and taking deep breaths, we remembered why we were there. The task at hand. We could actually win the Ivy League Championship that season.

We reminded ourselves that the next time we were with the whole team we had to tell the DRAVRAHOG story to the new freshmen so they understood our chant. And when we did, they loved it. It spoke to exactly who our team was. Passionate, energized, bold, creative but also self-deprecating and able to laugh at ourselves. We told them our history over the previous three years. They needed to understand how far we had come, how close we always were as a group and how close we had come to the title the previous year.

Preseason got under way with the Cooper test, and with a second new fitness test of a series of 120-yard sprints, we pushed each other with the constant and stoic reminder to "DO IT FOR BROWN."

When the time came for the talent show with the men's team, we arrived first. By the time the guys came in and sat down, we had already made ourselves comfortable, spreading ourselves out on the mats in the common room, and were laughing and talking loudly. Some of the boys looked nervous when they saw us. We *were* loud. A moment later we heard clapping and laughter coming from the men. They had egged on one of their freshmen to get up and dance at the front of the room. We were excited to see it too—if his senior teammates thought he had something, it had to be good. They were right. He danced in a way I'd never seen anyone dance before. It was so different, and really beautiful. I felt an electric zing. A powerful attraction. I'd never felt anything like it. One by one, people were also turning to see what was going on. Soon everyone was watching and the room got really quiet. I was reminded of the moment when I was a freshman and Flynnie took advantage of a quiet moment to yell out my new embarrassing nickname. Something came over me and I took the opportunity.

"SIDDOWN!" I laughed, yelling like a disgruntled spectator shouting at someone blocking their view at a game.

The boy froze and looked up at me with a surprised expression. My teammates followed my lead, laughing and heckling him to take a seat. He looked hurt and incredibly young. He really did look like a freshman. He was actually an adorable kid and I felt like a bully. I couldn't deny that when our eyes met I felt a jolt run through my body.

As he sat down, Mink nudged me: "That's the freshman named Armando. He's on the national team."

The freshman guys' main act of the night was a fake body-building contest. The guys made our freshmen rub body oil all over their freshmen and then the rest of us were supposed to clap for who we thought had the best body. But our six-foot blonde goalie—who had requested a badass-sounding nickname so we had taken to calling Sweet Pea—had zero interest in rubbing oil all over any man's body and instead ripped her shirt off like the Hulk and oiled her own six-pack. Our team sprang to our feet to give her a standing ovation, chanting her name: "Sweet Pea! Sweet Pea!"

Not long after that, she made us proud again. There had been a shift during my time at Harvard. When I started, the dating scene was still very binary, but not anymore, and we all loved it. Sweet Pea found her name at the top of the slutboard one day because she had approached a woman on the field hockey team at the Grille the night before and asked her out by saying: "Hey, I know we've showered together, but I've never formally introduced myself."

One evening a few days later at the Grille—after we had introduced our freshmen to the owners, Paul and Dave, and checked in on their first week according to our team tradition—Mink and I saw Armando and Will, one of the juniors on the men's team, walk into the Grille. The four of us ended up staying and hanging out after our freshmen all went back to their dorms. They were both quite funny. And the two of them literally toyed with people on the soccer field, which was pretty fun to watch. I'd never seen anything like it.

We were taking little good-natured jabs at each other about prospects for the upcoming season. Of course, the boys thought they were going to win an Ivy League title, but we thought we had the better chance and we explained exactly why: how close we had got the year before; how deep our squad was, especially having added some very talented freshmen again; how badass our goalies were, like the freshmen they'd seen for themselves at the talent show.

"All right then, if we win the Ivy League this year, you guys have to stand up on a table at the Grille and announce it to the whole place," Mink said.

Will sat back from the table, thinking for a second.

"We'll do it right here and now," he said, "if... if one of you kisses that girl over there."

He pointed to a girl sitting by the window with a friend.

I didn't hesitate. I jumped over the railing between my section of the bar and hers and strode over. As soon as I was on my way I started freaking out. *What had I done?* I had literally jumped at the chance to kiss a girl. It hit me pretty squarely and obviously that the dare to kiss a girl had been exciting to me. But this was a weird situation I'd put myself in. I also knew I couldn't back out. My pride and the pride of our team was on the line. That one moment was going to prove so many things: the profoundness of my confidence in my team; how far I was willing to go; how much I believed in us; and in a way how close us girls were. But I had to say something to this poor girl to convince her that I wasn't a crazy person. I needed to gain her trust by the way I approached her. I needed to convey that what I was asking her to do was important for womankind. What could I possibly say?

When I reached the table, I slowed down my approach and—with the most apologetic and pleading look on my face—I said to her: "Excuse me. Hi. I am *so* sorry to put you in this really awkward position, but is there any way it would be OK if I kiss you quickly so my friend and I can win a game of truth or dare with those guys over there?"

And I pointed at them. Luckily the looks of disbelief on their faces were comical. She had every right to shut me down. And I thought she might. But she looked at her friend and they both laughed. She said: "Sure."

So before I knew it, I was going in for a kiss. I touched my lips to hers. Her lips were soft and it was a sweet kiss. I definitely felt something in my whole body. Then I remembered to stand up. We looked each other in the eyes and both smiled. I brought my hands into prayer, bowed to her and said: "Thank you, thank you, thank you!" And I turned back to our table, where everyone was on their feet, Will and Armando were cheering wildly and Mink was laughing hysterically.

Mink started testing the strength of the table in a hammy way for the guys, and they knew what they had to do. They never hesitated, but both got up on the table and followed through on their end of the bet.

"Excuse me folks," Will began in a commanding voice. The regular week-night crowd in the bar had already turned to watch all the commotion. He started with a basic introduction, with one hand on his chest and the other on Armando's shoulder. "I'm Will and this is Armando and we just want to let everyone know... that... that..."

We were waiting. But he'd stopped. Instead of just saying it in the way that we were expecting—what our coach called "going through the motions," which would have been getting the announcement over with as quickly as possible and getting down off the table with minimal effort or emotion—he was taking a moment. We were trying to read his thoughts from the shifting expressions on his face. His body language changed, his arms outstretched, his smile wider and a genuine pride seemed to rise up on his face. He looked both surprised and empowered. It was like he was going from non-believer to believer right in front of our eyes. We had convinced him! Before he started to speak, it was clear that he was about to be completely sincere and actually emotional. He took a deep breath, looked out at the whole crowd and spoke to them all from his heart. He belted out:

"... that THE HARVARD WOMEN'S SOCCER TEAM IS GOING TO WIN THE IVY LEAGUE CHAMPIONSHIP THIS YEAR!"

The two boys raised their arms in the air and the whole place erupted into applause.

That night, a beautiful friendship was born. Will and Bing, one of our talented and gorgeous freshmen, were falling in love, and the five of us started hanging out all the time.

Things were also better with my sister too. We had decided to live together, with another friend, in a suite with three singles and a shared bathroom. We left a set of paints out for anyone who came over, using our plain wooden coffee table as a reusable canvas. And Katie had a parakeet named Merlin that flew free around the apartment and was most often perched on top of the television.

Sometimes after training, Mink, Bing and I would head to the boys' dressing room in the other building and then walk up to dinner with them. I was surprised how much nicer their building was and how much nicer their dressing room was than ours.

———

We got off to an ass-kicking start, beating Fairfield 2-0, Canisius 9-0, Maine 2-0, and Holy Cross 4-0. Stauffy was the leading scorer despite the fact that her brother Matt had been diagnosed with leukemia at the end of preseason. It was incomprehensible what was happening to him, to their family. Matt had been at Williams College where he was playing on the soccer team—a leader, of course, and inspiring his teammates there the same way he had inspired me when I first met him. Initially Stauffy went home but ultimately she decided to stay in school and keep playing with the team. She wouldn't approve of this language, but there's only one way to say it: Stauffy played her fucking guts out for us that season. And we played our fucking guts out for her in return.

We were scoring goals from all over the field, with everyone getting in on the action. Mink had two two-goal games. I managed to contribute an assist and a goal against Holy Cross. About halfway through the season, we lost a non-Ivy League match to Monmouth by a goal, but we came back to rout our cross-town rival Boston College 6-1.

Before home games, a few of us spray-painted a crimson "H" on Ohiri Field in the middle of the night. The first time we tried it, when we went back to look at it in daylight from the sideline the next day, it looked like a capital "I" instead of a Harvard "H." We joked that it was an "I" for "Idiots."

Tim was starting Stauffy and me in the center together, with her in the attacking role. I was playing my new role and my new style and even scored a couple of goals, but Bing had quickly proved she could play my position. She was young and fresh and healthy and very good. I hadn't played a full game since before my injury during my sophomore season. In previous games, I had waited for my quad to totally give out, and then still waited for Tim to notice and substitute me. Not anymore. During my senior season, I started raising my hand to signal for a sub before my quad gave out. Sometimes I didn't make it to halftime.

Coming out of games used to kill me; all I could think about was how to get back in again. But by that time I was fully grateful to have players on the team who could carry us further than I could, and I finally embraced my place on the sideline with pride.

One day, as we were getting changed after a chilly training session, there was a knock on the dressing-room door. From the other side, I heard Tim say I had a phone call. I followed him to the payphone in the hall. I'd never seen anyone get a phone call at that payphone before. Before I got the receiver all the way to my ear, I could hear my brother Tom crying on the other end. I knew before he said it.

"Sooz," he choked. "Aaron's dead... He hanged himself."

Everything went black. I have no recollection of the rest of the conversation or what I might have said to try to comfort Tom in his grief. My head filled up with noise; my eyes stung and tears fell down my cheeks. I felt myself start to spiral into negative thoughts. I hung up and put my forehead against the cold chrome plate on the front of the payphone. I couldn't believe it. Matt's illness and now Aaron.

I stood there for a minute, on the edge of panic, before wiping my eyes and nose with my sleeves. I decided I didn't have to tell anyone. I decided I didn't want to bring this to the team. There was nothing anyone could do. And, most importantly, news like this would only make things harder for Stauffy, whose brother was fighting for his life.

I stayed in touch with Tom over the next few weeks, worrying about his state of mind. He told me to stay with the team.

A few days later, we boarded the bus for a twelve-hour trip to our first Ivy League match of the season at Cornell, which ended in a disappointing scoreless draw in extra time even though we had at least ten shots more than them in the first half. We stayed after our game to cheer for Will, Armando and the rest of the men's team, who lost a tough one 3-1. It was a long drive home from Ithaca for all of us.

The next Saturday, we took our frustrations out on Penn, beating them 6-1 for our first conference win. Our defense, led by Noonan, was nearly impenetrable. Our freshman keeper, Sweet Pea, was dominating, having stepped in for our starting keeper who was out with a bad shoulder injury.

After we beat Colgate the next day, we had thirty-nine goals as a team, the most in the Ivy League. Our next match was against Yale in New Haven. Both teams were in a position to win the title, so the game was critical. It was the biggest game of the season and also happened to be Noonan's twenty-first birthday. In the huddle before the game, Stauffy told her we were going to win it for her. We had to make that happen, for both of them.

Yale dominated the first few minutes of play until Stauffy—we had taken to calling her "Mustafa." a combination of Stauffy and the name of Mufasa in Disney's *The Lion King*, which had come out the year before —single-handedly took control of the match. About halfway through the first half, she intercepted a ball cleared by Yale's back line, whizzed by two defenders, faked right and struck the ball to the left past their diving keeper.

"YESSSSSS!" we roared in celebration. Our bench leapt up and joined us on the field as we all jumped on top of her in a huge pile right in Yale's eighteen-yard box. After that, Yale never really had another scoring chance. The match ended with us on top, 2-0. The men's team also won their game.

The multiple special occasions called for a super-sized celebration. After our standard post-match gathering at the Grille, someone suggested a streak to Harvard's pool. Stripping down to our underwear, we left our clothes in the arms of a smarter teammate and sprinted two blocks to the pool with the men's team trying to catch up.

Once we got there, one of the men's players sat on the edge of the pool, shaking his head sadly: "I can't believe you're all naked, and I'm so drunk

I won't remember it," he said. "It's not fair. It's really not fair."

A few of us attempted to play water polo, with others jumping off the diving platforms, until the Harvard police busted us. They made everyone who didn't escape walk over to get our IDs out of our clothes, which our teammate had shown up with. Three of our teammates were discovered hiding—not very well—on the high-dive board. I heard one officer radio to another: "I've got three more naked ladies; coming your way."

The season continued. We thrashed Princeton 7-0 and then squeaked by Dartmouth 3-2 to stay on top of the Ivy League. For the second year in a row, the conference title was going to be decided in the last game of the season against Brown. And this time, we had to face them on their home turf.

I really wanted Katie to be there. She hadn't come to any of our games yet that season, and I still thought she was pissed off that I had been voted captain and she hadn't. One night, from the basement computer room of Kirkland House, I decided to try out Pine, the email program that was brand-new on campus.

"Why did you decide not to play soccer this year?" I typed. "I should have asked you a long time ago. I'm sorry."

From a computer in the science building Katie wrote back immediately: "Because I had a bit of a mental and physical breakdown."

"What do you mean?"

"I felt pathetic and friendless and alone and miserable and sick and hurt and slightly insane and hopeless and homesick. My face hurt to smile."

I couldn't believe the words I was seeing on the screen.

"Oh my god," I wrote back. "We were going through the same thing."

Of course we were, I thought to myself. *Of course we were.*

"Character building?" she responded.

The emails went back and forth. Each time a new message popped into that archaic-looking inbox, I felt giddy. Finally, my sister and I were talking, albeit electronically.

"It would mean a lot to me to have you at the Brown game," I wrote.

"Of course!" she replied. "I would never have missed it! And Mom and Dad are coming! You guys better F them up!"

That was as close as she came to cursing.

———

The Brown game was cold and wet. The visitors' dressing room smelled like the muddy field, which was all torn up from a season of play. Anxious for the match, for once we dressed in near-silence, pulling our jerseys down over our stomachs, where we had written "Buck Frown" in permanent marker. I felt weathered and responsible and focused, like a sea captain. The team was my ship, my whole life. I had made a lot of mistakes as a person and as a teammate. But I took some comfort from knowing that I had never faltered in one area: my commitment to the team. I felt like I had been working my entire life for the next ninety minutes. The *Harvard Crimson* had it right: we were hungry, and it was feeding time.

We huddled in the middle of the dressing room before going out to the field, taking a collective breath to exhale some of our nerves. Noonan and I both spoke to the team. Noonan reminded everyone that this was our time, her powerful words ending with: "This is our moment and *no one* is going to take this away from us."

I continued where she left off.

"We were here in this same moment last year and we came up short. But today is different. We are going to win this today. We owe it to our seniors last year, who never got their Ivy Ring, to get this revenge and to all our teammates who came before us. We took a lot of punches this season and we never gave up. It only made us stronger. We worked for a full year to be right here, right now. We never stopped believing we would get here, and look what we did. We made it. We're here. And we all know there is no way they are going to take this away from us. Not today."

Bing pulled something out of her bag. She said she had prepared something to read before the game. Reading from a cut-out piece of white paper glued to red construction paper, she started to speak. She'd written a variation of the famous Walt Whitman poem:

Oh Captain, my Captain, the time has come at last,
When we will make up for the failures of the past.
The ring is just a game away, a battle to be won,
With our war cry DRAVRAHOG! we'll send them on the run.
Oh Captain, my Captain, you are our leader and our friend.
You will keep us up and keep us strong right until the end.
When that final whistle sounds its tune,
There is one more team we've left in ruin.
Oh Captain, my Captain, victory is in our hands.
We'll conquer Brown and look up in the stands,
With our new title, the winning stamp,
We will be the Ivy Champs.

A blinding roar of voices ensued, and over the top of it all Noonan and I yelled our customary countdown in unison: "3-2-1..."

"DRAVRAHOG!" the team shouted.

The sun went down and the lights came on as we went through our pre-match warm-ups. Parents and siblings and aunts and uncles crowded into the stands. My parents were sitting with Katie. I could see Mink's parents and her sister, Bing's parents and her little sister and brother. The women's basketball, lacrosse and field hockey teams were there. Matty and the men's lacrosse team. The men's basketball team. Our fans were everywhere.

"Look!" Mink shouted. "The guys are here!"

I turned to see the men's team marching in from the car park in double-line formation with Will and Armando at the front. As they got closer, we could hear their chant:

"What's the color of shit?" one line yelled.

"Brown! Brown! Brown!" the other line responded.

In the huddle, Tim announced my name as a starter. He and I looked at each other. We both knew this was my final game. I'd made it. I wiped away my tears. We both knew my presence on the field was going to be short.

By the time the ref was ready to blow his whistle for kick-off, the men's team had assembled as a group standing in the bleachers, with a new crisp chant: "This is our Crim-son Ar-my!" they roared over and over, alternating with crisp beats of clapping: *Clap Clap. Clap-Clap-Clap.* Tears came again. This was all I ever wanted—to be enveloped in the heart of the game.

Then the game started, and there was no more time for tears. Brown came out fighting. We knew the match meant as much to them as it did to us and we didn't expect anything less.

About twenty minutes in, there was a scramble near Brown's goal. Players were falling over in the mud in their attempts to shoot or clear the ball as it ricocheted around. Noonan crashed into the box all the way from her position in the center of our defense. Coming from so far away, her momentum and perspective gave her an edge. Not mired in the mud, she got to the ball quicker than everyone else and struck. It was in.

Our fans went wild. We went wild. We ran at Noonan, screaming with our arms in the air and pummeled her from all sides, ending up in a big heap of muddy bodies. The ref blew his whistle and pointed to the center spot. We were 1-0 up. But there was a lot of time left, and we had been here before.

Some of Brown's fans had gathered behind our goal and began to pound on drums in an attempt to distract our keeper until the ref made them move away. Just before half-time, Brown almost equalized, beating us badly on a quick counterattack and sending their fans into a frenzy.

That was it. I knew it was time to make my exit. We needed Bing. She would be able to hold the middle. She was taller and stronger than any of Brown's players, and her skill and intimidating presence would contain them. It was time for Bing to take over from me for good.

I was finally facing the moment I'd been fending off for three long years, hampered by an injury that just never let me go. *The end.* I was relieved I'd made it to this point and hadn't given up. This was the right time now and I could let it go.

At the next stoppage in play, I knelt down and raised my hand. I bowed my head and closed my eyes to enjoy that last moment in my kit, shinpads, socks and beaten-up cleats, muddy and dripping with rain and sweat, with wet grass all over my face and savoring the beautiful smells of the game. The ref blew his whistle and called for the sub. I had to press down with my hands in the mud. Standing up hurt. I allowed some relief that it was finally all over to wash over me. As I walked off the field, I couldn't help but will myself—call it spirit or energy or soul, whatever—to release and lift away from my body to stay in the game with my girls.

As I walked off the field that last time, I was overwhelmed with gratitude that my teammates had been there for me all those times when I wasn't able to get up, fighting the fight while I was down. By the time of that match against Brown University, I had spent four years chasing that title and three years trying to heal from an unhealable injury. I had broken down, inevitably. It was through teammates and the structure of the team that I found a safety net and something bigger than myself. In those final moments, it all flashed before my eyes: the naivety, the pain, the struggle, the tears, the frustration, the self-loathing, the perseverance, the final achievement.

I knew I was part of something special both on and off the field. We were a group I couldn't be more proud to be part of—a small part of a much greater history—and, on top of all that, we had made it to the biggest battle. We were fighting with honor, as had been our core culture throughout our program's short history. That year, things had come together on the field with the right players, the right preparations and the right strategies, but we still needed our strength to hold out, and that last—sometimes painfully elusive—bit of luck.

The second half of the game was evenly matched. Stauffy and Bing were unbreakable in our midfield but Brown had no gaps in their defense so we couldn't get in behind them. But, having learned from the previous year, we never lost our focus. It was a back-and-forth battle.

I was standing on the sidelines, bouncing up and down a little unsteadily. I had my hands on two of my teammates' shoulders. I was favoring my right leg, but I needed their support more emotionally than physically. We were buzzing with fearful hope and bottled-up kinetic energy, barely staying off the field, leaning in, begging for the clock to tick down faster. We strained to see where the ball was going, willing it to stay at our team's feet, praying that an opportunity for a last-second "Hail Mary play" near our goal wouldn't suddenly appear like it had the year before.

"Blow the whistle!" we were screaming at the referee. *"BLOW IT!"*

We were alternating between watching the ball and the referee, desperate for him to raise his whistle to his mouth.

When the whistle eventually blew, we had done it. We had finally beaten Brown and won the Ivy League Championship.

I watched my teammates sprint from the sideline and all over the field to pile on Noonan again, our captain who had scored the winning goal in her final game to win the title. I was one of the last to arrive. I didn't jump on the pile. I laid myself down carefully on top, feeling all the bodies beneath me, listening to the muffled voices of triumph and savoring every second, just like my dad had taught me. All around us, there was whooping and hollering, flags and scarves waving, people hugging and high-fiving, cameras flashing.

After we got back to our feet, I found myself next to Noonan. I put my hand out, and she took it. I looked at her, smiling. When the tears started to fall from my eyes, she pulled me in for a hug.

———

I knew my career was done, but some of my teammates had finished their college careers still at the top of their game. They had so much more to offer. So much talent. At the time, there was no professional women's soccer league. The professional women's basketball league in the US was still a year away. I heard that my old club teammate Erin Martin had gone to play in a league in Australia after graduating from Stanford, and I heard a few others had gone to Sweden. That was exciting but we all wanted an option for them at home. Those girls were true pioneers; there was no path to follow. They were bravely blazing trails into a future for women's professional soccer.

Meanwhile, life went on for me. Or a version of my life without soccer, which didn't really feel like my life at all.

I filled most of my new-found free time with Armando. I had tried hard to smother the strong impulse I felt the first time I saw him. I'd never felt anything like it before so I didn't know what it was. All I knew was that I was a senior and he was a freshman; anything besides platonic camaraderie was outside the realm of possibility. Because of the age difference, we never had to deal with any expectation from ourselves or anyone else that we would become a couple. With that pressure off the table, we were able to hang out as friends, which was good because I wanted to be near him.

The friendship that developed between us was one of the easiest friendships I'd ever made. At first we only hung out with the group, Will, Bing and Mink. Then we started studying together on our own. He and I were so close that he would tell me about the girls he was dating or wanted to date or thought were hot, and sometimes I would agree. We'd been palling around together, in total denial of the affection that was growing between us. One day we were doing economics homework together in Annenberg Hall and I looked up at him. I felt like I wanted to hold his hand. But I kept pushing that feeling away.

Eventually, in the spring of his freshman year—my senior year—the reality of my upcoming graduation hit. I had always assumed I would go home to California after I finished at Harvard. But now that thought made me sad instead of excited. I wasn't ready to leave Armando behind. I wanted to keep seeing him every day. The fear of losing him made me finally drop the pretenses. One night at the Grille, I turned to Mink as Armando was getting us a drink and yelled over the loud music into her ear: "You're not going to believe this…"

"What?"

She couldn't hear me over the music. I thought about saying, "Never mind." It was so outrageous. No one would believe it. It could never work.…. But a feeling of giddy joy swelled up in my heart, and I knew in that moment that my love for Armando was real and like nothing else I'd ever felt before.

I put my hand on her shoulder, leaned in closer to her ear and started over in a louder voice.

"You're not going to believe this, but I think I have *feelings* for Armando."

There was a pause as she took in what I'd said. And then she let out a bellowing, happy laugh and gave me a big hug.

Things moved quickly after that. The next day he knocked on the door of my dorm room with a rose in his hand. A couple of days later he knocked on my door with my favorite pizza. A week later he made his mom's lobster sauce for us in the little, under-equipped kitchen in the basement of my dorm. It felt like a parachute had opened above me. He gave me what I needed. The kind of love that takes your headache away, your pain away, and leaves you feeling warm and happy.

One day I was flabbergasted by something he said to me.

"Once we have kids, everything we do will be for them," he said.

I didn't know what to say. We had only been together for a few weeks and he was only eighteen years old. Words flooded my mind. Like honor. Self-sacrifice. Fatherhood. Motherhood. Love. He was offering all of those things to me. It was real. And I could tell he meant it to be forever. All I had to do was say yes.

I pulled myself up in my tracks. This was a very different future to the one I'd been imagining for myself. The path I'd been on was headed toward an alternative lifestyle—I wasn't sure what that was going to look like yet but I knew I wasn't going to let society or anyone else tell me what I could or couldn't do. Life with Armando would be a traditional Catholic family unit: husband, wife and kids. Just how we had both grown up. It didn't feel like I was abandoning logic for passion. It felt familiar and safe and exciting. I thought I could have both.

I grasped his hand and embraced his vision for the two of us building a family together.

"Yes." I said, feeling like the love was so strong that it would make everything else work out. "Yes."

A few days later, my family flew from California to Boston to see Katie and I graduate from Harvard. My dad got choked up and cried openly in the hotel room as he was giving a champagne toast, unable to get his words out or stop the tears. Once he was able to speak he looked at the two of us and spoke the most sentimental words I'd ever heard him say: "I'm just so happy and proud of you both. My daughters. This is just an… an unbelievable day. I love you. Thank you for all of the wonderful memories. Your mother and I, we have enjoyed every second. We really have. Congratulations, both of you."

He lifted his glass to us. Everyone raised their glasses with a happy "cheers" and I took a sip of champagne mixed with a big salty tear that slid in at the edge of my mouth.

PART 3

TO NY AND BEYOND

I loved that my soccer career ended with a big win like a storybook ending, but after soccer and college were over I was in unscripted territory and it didn't feel good at all. I had a degree from Harvard but—not unlike many college students—I had graduated with a degree in a field where there wasn't a clear path to a paying job. The jobs I was qualified for were unpaid internships in the emerging environmental sector. My dad had been right. I had to face the fact that trusting my gut hadn't paid off.

After more than two decades of almost constant physical activity, my body was adjusting to life without soccer. There was a lot of "blah" without the daily doses of endorphins. I wasn't even really trying to find a substitute as I didn't think anything could ever match up. The lights in my life turned on when I was out on the field and now they'd shut back off. My heart and mind had to adjust to life as a civilian and life without the team.

By the mid-nineties, most people recognized that the prince-saves-the-princess pattern in fairy tales was not what we wanted to be teaching our little girls any longer, but the messaging had been implanted. There was a little girl inside me who enjoyed the narrative in which Armando played the part of my prince charming. He was rescuing me from the feeling of not belonging anywhere anymore and the boredom of life without soccer.

I'd fallen in love with a boy, but I had a residual mistrust of the whole gender. I felt some anger lurking beneath the surface and, without soccer as a release, I unfairly took some of that aggression out on him.

As, in my halting way, I learned to accept his kindness and be kind back to him in the consistent way required in a real relationship, he stayed with me. Eventually I learned I could trust him, and we started to feel like a team.

I had always planned to go home to California after graduation, and Armando agreed to come and spend the summer before his sophomore year with me. But we didn't end up staying very long. My dad wasn't comfortable with Armando and didn't want him around. Armando was the threat he'd been afraid of. The threat of the East Coast. I'm not sure he would have been comfortable with any boy I brought home unless maybe he was a Stanford football player businessman from Southern California. Meanwhile, Armando's family wanted him home and he felt guilty, so we drove back and spent the rest of the summer in New York.

The house that Armando had grown up in was a special place. It was the soccer home I'd dreamed of as a little girl. The television was always tuned to soccer. A signed Pelé ball was displayed in a glass box on top of the china cabinet—where, in my family's house, my mother displayed her rotating holiday decorations. Armando's three younger siblings and their teammates were always playing soccer both inside and outside the house. His mom made loads and loads of pasta every evening, managing the kitchen in the middle of all that chaos with her beautiful smile and endless energy.

I remember sitting on the family couch one weekend afternoon, squeezed in between Armando and his dad, watching Italian soccer on the television while his mom and aunt prepped their sauce, chatting quietly in their native language in the kitchen. Tears filled my eyes, and I started to cry. It was a quiet, happy, it's-all-going-to-be-OK cry. I thought: *This could be my new team. I could be happy doing this for the rest of my life.* After a little while, though, I realized I needed to go and help in the kitchen. In my house when I was growing up, most of the time my dad and brothers helped with the dishes and my mom sat down with us to watch sports. Thinking back, it had been pretty equal and I liked it that way.

This was the summer of 1996, the year the summer Olympics were

132

held in Atlanta, Georgia. Women's soccer was set to make its Olympic debut, whereas men's soccer had been in the Olympics for a hundred years already. *A century. We had been left out for a century.* It was a heavy thought. I was thrilled for the girls coming up behind me—including Armando's sisters, just twelve and sixteen at the time—who would have an opportunity to be in the Olympics. But finding out that boys had had that opportunity for a hundred years was like a punch in the gut.

That year was a real turning point for women's soccer in the United States. The US women's national team had threatened to boycott the games in Atlanta over a dispute about pay. The information available was vague, but it was the first time I thought that maybe the experience of the national team wasn't everything I'd been imagining. Foudy was the captain, so I trusted that the team had good reasons to do what they were doing. I knew they were playing for the love of the game and pride of our country, not for money. They wouldn't be rocking the boat if they didn't feel they had to.

These girls were my people. I wanted to live the Olympic dream with them. I wanted to see them beat their nemesis, Norway, in the semifinal in front of 65,000 fans in Georgia, to see Foudy give the ball to MacMillan for the winning goal, and then to watch them beat China 2-1 in the final to win the first ever Olympic gold medal in women's soccer in front of 80,000 ardent women's soccer fans. The problem was, the games weren't televised. I didn't get to see any of it.

That autumn, Armando went back to school for his sophomore year. It was an easy decision to move back to Boston with him. I looked for somewhere to live, crashing in his dorm room in the meantime. I was feeling inadequate and unsure of myself. My classmates were taking jobs in finance and consulting at companies like Putnam, Fidelity, Goldman Sachs, Merrill Lynch, J.P. Morgan and Morgan Stanley. Some of my teammates were already in medical or law school. I was floundering.

I applied for work at a temp agency. The woman who interviewed me—matching me up with an architecture firm where I was responsible for administrative support for a team of architects who were working on a public school north of Boston—made me feel better, sort of.

"You know you're overqualified for this job," she said.

"Thank you," I answered.

I knew on paper I looked qualified but I didn't feel qualified for any job, let alone overqualified.

When I finished my work at the firm and found myself sitting in front of a computer with free time, I started typing notes about our team. We were a bit *Bad News Bears* meets *Animal House*. I found that whenever I was writing about soccer, it was like I was right back in it. And oh, how I loved being back in it, even if just in my own mind, so I indulged myself every afternoon.

Unfortunately, Armando wasn't having the best experience on the men's team. The situation with their coach had gone from bad to worse. Instead of suffering through it, he withdrew from school. Against the wishes of both sets of our parents, we decided to move to Italy for a year. He worked as a waiter for the summer and made twice as much money as I had at my job at the architecture firm, which gave us enough money to live off of as long as we budgeted properly. He was exact with our budget. I teased him about it but I loved it and realized I was lucky he was sensible with our money because I wasn't.

We lived on a tight budget in the house of a family friend on the outskirts of Rome and took the bus into the city to take classes. (Our parents' reluctant acceptance of our plan came with the condition that we would study at a nearby university.) Armando trained and played with a local soccer team to stay in shape for his eventual return to Ohiri Field, and at first I went with him. It was too hard for me to sit out; I missed it too much. I figured I would play until it hurt. I was hoping that maybe playing on a small field would make it less likely that I would aggravate my torn quadricep.

At Harvard, the men's and women's teams had operated with a lot of mutual respect. We played pick-up games together and cheered each other on. We understood that our commitment to the game was the same: we worked out in the same gym, practiced on the same field, faced the same challenges in balancing our sport with studies. At least that's what I believed.

In Italy, it was different. I soon found out that the Italian men weren't used to women playing soccer. I had a hint of this at Armando's house. His sisters were the only girls of all the cousins to play, but all the boy cousins played. In Italy the men allowed me to join in at the beginning of their sessions, but when it was time to actually play the game, they got serious, patted me on the back and waited for me to get off the field. I was hurt but not sure how to respond. Armando didn't seem to think anything was wrong with their assumption that I wouldn't play in their games, and I lacked the confidence to insist on sticking around. After a while, I stopped going.

———

We spent nine months in Italy, getting to know Rome inside out, hosting friends and family, and eating like pigs: the square-cut pizza wrapped in tidy white paper; the wide, flat, extra-long ciabatta that we ate on the bus ride home; the cheeses; the pastas and the sauces we'd never tasted before. But we also missed home. Stauffy lost her brother while we were gone, and I missed the funeral. I felt bad that I hadn't been there for my friend, and Armando and I both knew we had real lives to get back to, to build both individually and together.

Armando had to go back to school. Neither of us wanted me to go all the way back to California to live with my parents, but I was broke. It seemed like the only option until Armando did something bold. He built me a bedroom in his parent's basement so I could live inexpensively while I looked for a job in New York City. I already felt so close to his family that the situation didn't even seem strange to me.

I was still interested in technology despite my decision to pass on computer science as a freshman, so when I saw a job advertised at a software consultancy firm in New York City I was excited. The company was looking for people to help troubleshoot issues with the so-called Y2K bug that everyone was expecting to wreak havoc on computer systems at the stroke of midnight on New Year's Eve the following year, but I didn't tick any of the qualification boxes so I was nervous and insecure at the interview. Luckily, the manager asked me the one question I felt confident to answer in the affirmative: was I ready for the hard work and sharp learning curve that was required for the job? I felt like he was a coach for a team I was trying out for. If he gave me a chance, I knew I could provide what he was looking for.

"I know what hard work is, sir, and I'm ready to commit myself to something new," I said. I took a quick breath, feeling the way I used to when I convinced a coach to let me take a penalty. "I am *absolutely* ready for this, sir."

Later he told me in front of a large group of our coworkers that he'd been very impressed with my enthusiasm and confidence in the interview. It felt just as good as getting recognized in the dressing room after a job well done on the field.

I rose up the ladder at work more quickly than I'd expected. I liked being a Shmennie again. I arrived early and stayed late, just like being first on and last off the field when required to carry the cones and bibs for our team. The company offered free classes on the weekends, and I took as many as I could: Java, JavaScript, Fireworks, Dreamweaver, Flash and many of the early web-design tools. I was in that rebuilding mode again, trying to prove myself, preparing for a future championship match.

I started to see a way that I might be valuable again and eventually able to support myself. I enjoyed going to work the same way I'd enjoyed going to training. I felt productive and liked my work team. I was grateful every day for my new job. After six months of steady paychecks, I tried to get Armando's parents to let me pay rent. It didn't work.

That summer, I used my time off to fly home to California. The United States was hosting the FIFA Women's World Cup games at the Rose Bowl and my mom had tickets to the final match.

The atmosphere in Pasadena around the 1999 FIFA Women's World Cup was as exciting as the 1995 FIFA Women's World Cup in Sweden. In fact, because the games were in the NFL football stadiums, it felt more like the atmosphere in Pasadena around the 1994 FIFA Men's World Cup. It was a dream: the giant stadium, my home turf, all my heroes fighting for the Cup. It felt enormous. It felt bigger than the game. We—me and the team and all of us who loved them—were fighting for more than just the World Cup. We were fighting to stake our claim in the upper echelons of the sporting hierarchy.

The final between the US and China delivered the epic showdown to cap off the record-smashing tournament, complete with Cold War-level tensions between our two countries (the US military had bombed the Chinese Embassy in Yugoslavia, killing three people just weeks before). Every game was broadcast live on television.

It was a sweltering day and the game was scoreless. Near the end of the second half, star midfielder Michelle Akers—who'd had a dozen knee surgeries by that time in her career and was playing with chronic fatigue syndrome and a dislocated shoulder—hit the ground after a blow to the head from the fists of charging Brianna Scurry. Wincing, we felt the impact all the way from our seats. It was a bad head injury, and they had no choice but to take her off. Losing Akers was like losing the queen in a game of chess. She had always been impossible to contain on the attack, and had led the team to the 1991 World Cup Championship with ten goals including the winner in the final. Recently she had slid back to a more defensive role. She was the most dominant player in the history of the American team. The big question now was whether the team could fend off the re-energized China attackers—including Sun Wen, who was in the lead for the Golden Boot—without their five-foot-ten lioness? It was anyone's game. The team scrapped, clawed and held on, and the game remained 0-0 through extra time, thanks in no small part to a legendary defensive header off the goal line by Kristine Lilly.

In the brief period between the end of extra time and the first penalty kick, none of the 90,185 spectators (the largest crowd to ever watch a women's sporting event) sat down in the giant Rose Bowl, including President Bill Clinton. The stress of each penalty was like nothing I'd ever experienced before. I witnessed Brianna Scurry's miraculous save and the lead-up to Brandi Chastain's winning penalty, not finding out until years later that she'd taken it with her left foot although she was right-footed. She'd switch-kicked—not something soccer players normally do, unlike baseball players—to throw off the Chinese coaching staff and goalkeeper to win the biggest moment in sport.

The 1999 Women's World Cup had clearly been a success. It was definitely a success for FIFA, who had never had to pay prize money for any of the women's world cups. The news said over 40 million households in the United States alone tuned in to the final. The maverick team became known as the 99ers, and I hoped that women's soccer and soccer in general in America had finally broken through. But eventually it started to feel like the mainstream sports media had just acquiesced to share space that summer, appeasing the appetite but refusing a sustained change. The sports pages returned to their daily routines despite the report by ESPN that two-thirds of the TV viewers who'd watched the Women's World Cup were men.

But the market was proven and the players were able to find enough support and investment to build the Women's United Soccer Association (WUSA). Women were finally afforded an opportunity to play in a national professional league. It was eye-opening for me to hear reports that this was the first fully professional women's soccer league in the world. I had just assumed there were successful leagues in other parts of the world, where soccer was more popular, where women were living the life of a professional soccer player, *living the dream.* Seeing so many players from around the world at the top of their game was inspiring but I had started to wonder where they were playing—how they were playing at that level if it wasn't a full-time, well-compensated job. How were they doing it?

My teammates began getting opportunities to play in the WUSA. I could only imagine what that felt like. But the initial thrill was weighed down by the reality.

Stauffy had returned to school, after taking the year off to be with her brother and family around the time of his tragic passing, and extraordinarily she led the team to its fourth Ivy Championship in five years. After graduating, she won a highly sought-after position at a non-profit called Teach for America that trains young teachers and places them in schools in low-income communities. But the WUSA wanted her. She was torn. She had already started teaching third grade at a public school in Jersey City, New Jersey. She knew she couldn't leave behind the children in her classroom. She also had her career path to think about; the positions at Teach for America were extremely hard to get, and as passionate as she was about soccer, the league's future was uncertain. Professional soccer wasn't a dependable career choice yet, though we thought it would be in just a few more years. But she wasn't being offered enough money to support herself now, and there was a risk that she could get injured and then have to reenter the workforce after her classmates, having fallen behind in experience and momentum.

Armando graduated from Harvard in May 2000 and took a job in finance in San Francisco. I was able to transfer with my company, so we moved west, into a two-bedroom apartment with Mink, my best friend from school, who had transferred by coincidence from New York to San Francisco for a big job with her company. My family was happy that we were on the West Coast and in familiar territory, although several hours north, and I was thrilled to reconnect with so many girls I had known through soccer over the years.

With Mink, a group of us got together to form a women's team at the historic Olympic Club, which had only started allowing female members in 1990, two years after the club admitted its first black men. I was so excited to get back on the field. But ten minutes into my first outdoor game since college, my quad injury resurfaced and I limped off.

I couldn't help but keep trying. The ball felt too good at my feet, even in my hands. I had always loved the feel of the stitching, spinning a ball around in my palms, bumping it against my shoulders or chest. I had another chance to play in a coed indoor league. Playing in a small gymnasium protected my leg. I didn't have to make any long passes that would have strained my quad. I had a good run playing in that league —full of drippy, sweaty high-fives, so many goals and assists, so many sprints back into defense, all the satisfaction the game had to offer.

When we moved farther downtown and there wasn't an indoor coed league near us anymore, I turned to running again. I ran before work or after work, trying to avoid the steepest sections of San Francisco's beautiful, hilly neighborhoods. I was on one of my early-morning runs, on September 11, 2001, when the news came through on my headphones that there had been an explosion at the World Trade Center buildings in New York City. Mink worked for Merrill Lynch and was in New York, scheduled to fly home that morning. I didn't yet know what had caused the explosion in the tower, but I knew it couldn't be good. I broke into a sprint.

I got home, turned on the television and watched in horror as the North Tower fell.

I felt the emptiness of Mink's bedroom to my left. Normal routines stopped, and no stores opened. Friends came over and we sat together, watching the devastating images, waiting for news of what had happened and why.

When we finally heard from Mink, she told us she'd been in a hotel across the street, scheduled to fly home on United Airlines Flight 93 from Newark to San Francisco, the highjacked flight that crashed in a field in Pennsylvania. But she'd missed the flight, having slept right through her alarm after staying up late watching *Monday Night Football* with some New York City friends. I'd never heard of Mink missing anything she was scheduled to do or attend.

The randomness of her survival was haunting. So many people, including so many of her friends and colleagues, *had* gone to work that day. Mink didn't come home for weeks, first because all the airports were shut down, then because she stayed for funeral after funeral after funeral. My once happy, carefree pal did eventually come home to us; we did our best to help her with her healing process.

Armando and I knew we needed to visit his family in New York. We needed to touch the ground there, in solidarity. We needed to hug them all in person.

We were able to go to New York just before the winter holidays. Our time with his family was always special, but this time was even more so. We always stayed up late when we were there, but this time we stayed at the dinner table even longer and we held each other closer. Armando's aunt told us how she had walked all the way home, twelve miles, from Manhattan that day with thousands of other people.

We wanted to do something more to support the city. Tourism had gone down, hotels and restaurants were struggling. Armando decided to plan a night in the city for the two of us: a room at the Plaza, dinner and a show. On the night before Christmas Eve, we packed an overnight bag and headed in on the train. We went for a long run in Central Park, which I had never seen. I wanted to get back to the hotel and change for our fancy dinner, but Armando kept running, pulling over every so often to check out a gazebo or to look out over the water or stand beside a wooden bench. I'd never seen him nervous, ever, but that's exactly what he seemed like he was.

"What are you doing?" I yelled. "Let's go back! We've been running long enough!"

But Armando insisted that we continue until finally we reached a pretty little bridge. Before I could complain again, he got down on one knee in front of me and proposed. I started crying.

"Yes," I laughed. "Yes, yes, yes!"

We walked back to the Plaza, arm in arm. I was in a daze. It had happened—we were taking the next step. I was so ready for our future together, and all the more appreciative for the possibility because of the incomprehensible tragedy our country had just suffered.

When we left for the airport to go back to San Francisco everyone cried. It was hard to leave. I'd become very close to his family. His siblings had become my siblings; his parents were much more than future in-laws; they were my friends. But we had our own life back in California. I was about to start a new job as a junior systems administrator at a company called Pacific Data Imaging, or PDI, that had been acquired by DreamWorks and had just won the Academy Award for Best Animated Feature for *Shrek*. It was truly dream work for me. I'd been catching up on computer science classes on nights and weekends at a local adult continuing education center picking up a large Starbucks coffee on my way there every time to help me get through the long classes. I was hoping to transition into animation one day. I loved the idea of being able to tell stories without the confines of the real world.

I was also still working to put eggs in more baskets. I looked into the process of getting in to graduate school to get a master's degree in computer science. I loved my career in technology. The first step was taking the admissions exam for American graduate schools known as the GRE, short for the Graduate Record Exam. If I did well enough on the exam, I might be able to go back to school to open up more opportunities for myself. Plus, I just wanted to know more.

Initially I was afraid of committing to taking the test. I wasn't sure I could learn everything I had to learn, and failing was going to hurt. Being rejected from graduate schools was going to hurt. But I had a change of heart. I remembered the moment I'd had in college when I took organic chemistry and aced it—why hadn't that achievement stayed with me? Where had that confidence gone? Why had I let myself fall back into an insecure mindset? Why was it so hard for me to believe in myself? And on top of all that, what was so bad about failing anyway? Was I that weak that I was letting a little bit of hurt pride stop me from taking important chances? After seeing so many lives tragically cut short, I understood that life wasn't a certainty. Life is a gift not to be taken for granted, and I had to give it back my all, to go for my biggest dreams and earn my place.

Like I'd done with organic chemistry, I put my faith in the idea that practicing for a test was the same as practicing a sport, where hard work and time pay off. I was totally shocked when I got my score back. I did so well on the GRE that I got accepted to three graduate schools. I also appreciated the Harvard name on my application. I was getting accustomed to applying myself to achieving work goals the way I had done in soccer. It felt really good, and I was gaining confidence.

A year into my job at DreamWorks, I made a hard choice and decided to go back to school. I loved being part of a well-known movie studio—especially one owned by famous media giants like Spielberg, Katzenberg, and Geffen—but it wasn't all about me. Armando wasn't happy where we were. The finance world was still sorting itself out after the dot-com bubble had burst, and for the first time in his life Armando was adrift. I knew the feeling and, having another option for myself, was willing to make a sacrifice. My dad offered Armando a job with the family business in Los Angeles, so we moved back to the beach condo, he started learning the business and working in the warehouse, and we got married over the summer. I started school in the autumn.

It was the life I'd imagined for myself, back in Southern California, settling down. But it was about to slip away before the roots even took hold. My doctor had been concerned that my polycystic ovary syndrome would make it difficult for me to get pregnant, so she recommended I come off the pill right after our June wedding in my home town. Her concerns turned out to be unfounded: I was pregnant by January. The excitement and relief eclipsed all other priorities, and we dubbed our growing family our *Home Team*. I had constant nausea and vomiting, though, which made it impossible to sit through a class and made me think I might have to postpone school. At the same time, Mink's sister offered Armando an incredible job in New York.

It felt like the best decision for our family was for Armando to take the job in New York. It was the kind of opportunity that could give us real stability. I would get through the pregnancy and reevaluate my next step from there. Within six months, we were living in Manhattan.

———

We had our three children—a daughter and two boys—in five years. With help from both sets of parents, we were able to buy a house. We moved from our rented one-bedroom apartment in Manhattan eastwards to Queens and then a year later east again to Long Island. I handled the kids and the two moves while Armando was working long hours; we'd divided up the labor, and a new plan for our family's future was taking shape. It was a rebuilding period.

Those hectic years passed by and I chose to focus on being a mom. As

I'd hoped when we moved from California, Armando's job was worth the cross-country move and I didn't feel any pressure to go back to work right away. I did miss the learning but I never really considered going back to school as paying for school and childcare would have been too expensive. I did consider going back to work—I missed my exciting career—but the reality of it made me anxious. Taking on more than I was already doing was daunting. The process of finding and then paying for full-time childcare didn't seem worth it if I was only going to break even with my salary. Commuting with either morning sickness or while breastfeeding was intimidating. Our daughter, Madi, was facing a unique set of health issues and I was afraid to not be with her. Rationally I knew women overcame those obstacles all the time, but I wished for a way to make it work and felt very lucky Armando's job paid our bills while I tried to figure it out.

If I had a spare few minutes I found myself picking up my writing again. I wrote a journal on my laptop—everything from trying to be a good mother to frustrations with my husband for constantly making me clean up after him to light-hearted humor about integrating into a very large, first-generation Italian family. I remember thinking: *Wouldn't it be amazing if I could somehow make a living by doing this?* It was a totally crazy dream—I'd never excelled at writing and had studied only science in college—but if I could figure it out I would be able to work from home where I was feeling like I needed to be.

One of the first things I did once my youngest son was in school was go to a women writers' conference in New York City. There I met a woman named Jane who was trying to fill a gap in the market by publishing young adult books for and about young female athletes. Until then I hadn't realized that I'd never had a book to read about someone like me, and I thought of Madi not having books to read about girls like her.

I told Jane about my interest in writing and my background in soccer and she asked me: "Why aren't *you* writing about sports?"

And I just looked at her, dumbfounded.

A chance meeting, a serendipitous conversation, a simple question, prompted a profound change in my path. Over the next few weeks, I began pulling out my old notes that I'd written about our team. I also started trying to educate myself about what good sports writing looked like. I knew I had a lot to learn if I wanted to produce something worth people's time and attention.

I started by reading popular sports books like *Fever Pitch* by Nick Hornby and I also found the dark *A Fan's Notes* by Frederick Exley. Then I found a series published annually called *The Best American Sports Writing.* Jane was right: the stories were about male sports and written by men. Then I looked back at the list of classic and beloved sports movies—*Hoosiers, Rocky, Chariots of Fire, Rudy, Bad News Bears, The Natural, Field of Dreams, Major League, Remember the Titans, The Sandlot, Miracle,* and my personal childhood favorite *Escape to Victory.* Men's sports with male directors.

I had to dig deeper than my usual media diet to find women's sports. Surprised, I found a documentary called *Dare to Dream* about the history of the 99ers. I'd heard the names before: Anson Dorrance, Mia Hamm, Kristine Lilly, Brandi Chastain, Joy Fawcett, Julie Foudy, and Michelle Akers. But the documentary filled in gigantic gaps in the story. Even those of us so closely a part of it didn't know what they'd gone through or the way their story fits into the greater history of women's sports, with the individual athletes fighting for their right to play one by one before any team sports developed.

I became aware of all the girls throughout history who just wanted to be free and run around like the boys, to play a sport they loved, but being told no over and over again. How brave they must have been. How desperate and determined they must have been. They'd followed their hearts and demanded the right to play and compete. How lonely that must have been. My eyes filled with tears. It's so hard to swim up river all the time. I wanted to know the history—I wanted to know who all those girls and women were. They had blazed the trail that I arrived on. They were my predecessors. Without them I wouldn't have had my place in the game. I wouldn't have had my opportunities. Without them I wouldn't have had *my life.* This new perspective was in my blood, flowing through my brain and body for the first time, changing every cell. I hadn't appreciated the hard work of the girls and women who had come before me.

It was the first time I heard from the players what their experience was like. Michelle Akers said that when they went to China for what I'd known as the first women's world cup, FIFA "didn't feel confident that they were going to put on a good enough show for it to be a FIFA-sanctioned World Cup. So it was sort of, 'We'll call it this and if it works out good, you guys can be the FIFA World Cup the next time around.'" Wait, *what?!* FIFA didn't believe in us from the beginning? Why *not?* And what was the name they came up with? The FIFA Women's World Championship for the M&M's Cup.

The truth was devastating. And like tumbling dominoes, more hard truths were finally falling and were impossible to stop. All I could do was stand back and watch them all fall where they may.

The women's team was treated differently than the men's team. The United States Soccer Federation (US Soccer) assumed that the men's national team was going to be the team that made a name for the United States in soccer, not the new women's team, so that's where the money and resources went. US Soccer also told the women's coach—Anson Dorrance, the architect of the women's program and the team—that if the team didn't perform well in China he would be fired. *Fire Anson Dorrance? The greatest coach in American soccer?* No wonder the team rallied together. They were fighting for their beloved and intrepid leader.

I had to get this all straight in my head. US Soccer was the organization I'd had up on a pedestal for creating a women's national team program. The organization I'd respected as genius in how they carefully and thoughtfully selected the most talented coach and players in the country, putting together a team and the beginnings of a youth system that had single-handedly brightened my outlook on life and given me a healthy lifelong goal to aspire to. The organization I had assumed was equally proud of me and all the female players bursting with pride to represent their state, region—and, if they were lucky, their country—with everything we had, just as they were proud of their boys.

I'd believed that US Soccer was the best of what America was all about. Equal opportunity for all.

I was nauseous.

The team traveled without getting paid, and their parents scraped the money together for the trips. Grateful and excited for their opportunities, they were just happy to be playing the game they loved with people they cared about. They were willing to do anything to get to the top. And that they did. But women's soccer was still considered a hobby.

A section of *Dare to Dream* told the story of Joy Fawcett's return to the team just three weeks after having her baby. Anson let her bring the baby on the road. She was able to breastfeed her baby and stay on the team. The other players loved having Joy and her baby with them and she had two more children while playing for the team. She made her career and motherhood work. She made it work, but also the team made it work. Pioneers, leaders, role models—it was incredibly inspiring.

Another powerful moment in the documentary was when a journalist covering the 1995 World Cup in Sweden spoke about the experience of the tournament: "It was a beautiful country and it was a great event, but… but nobody cared." My heart sank. Is that how it was perceived? I had cared. My mom and I had cared. We were there and we weren't alone. There was a magic in the air; it was a beautiful vibe. Had the media been making the team feel like no one cared? Now I felt even worse about not showing up at that after-party and wearing my heart on my sleeve, displaying my passion and love and respect for the team for all of them to see and feel. Sharing it with them. But I'd been too shy, too chicken. *They* had needed *me*. Little old me—a fan from home, one of their disciples and supporters, willing to travel any distance to be with them and witness their story and join their movement. My one voice would have mattered a lot.

It was also good for me to see how intense they were. It was good for me to see that it was OK to be that fiercely competitive. It was OK to use the word revenge. It was OK to want to punch a photo of the other team. It was OK to care that much.

The documentary explained how Mia Hamm became the face of the team and how companies started using her in advertising campaigns. Paying a trendy or beloved athlete to endorse a brand was a marketing strategy that had always worked, but major advertisers had not recognized a female soccer player as a powerful endorser until Mia. Her endorsements (a national shampoo brand, Nike and Pepsi, among others) had important ripple effects and proved that investment in marketing campaigns with female soccer players paid off.

And then hearing the real story of the contract disputes starting with the 1996 Olympics. The American tennis legend Billie Jean King explained how she became friends and allies with Julie Foudy and her team. King had shared with Foudy her story—how she had united her peers in professional women's tennis and created their own Women's Tennis Association. Talking and negotiating with tennis officials hadn't worked. Uniting was the only way to progress toward equal respect and pay. US Soccer wasn't providing equitable support for the women's team in general—travel, meals and pay were different. Talking and negotiating hadn't worked for them either. Foudy recognized it was the same situation. The soccer team was going to have to follow King's lead and unite. They needed to force change to get what they deserved. It was unfortunate but it was the only way. They were going to have to refuse to play as a team— strategic boycotts. It was the only leverage they had.

Not only did I learn about King's critical role, but I also learned about Donna de Varona and her unfaltering leadership as the head of the 1999 World Cup organizing committee. She was a game-changer in women's history but, like so many of our heroes, her story was still untold.

Meanwhile, my passion for the game found a new outlet. My sister-in-law Teresa and I began talking about starting a coaching business. Like me, she had a young daughter and had played soccer in college. We wanted to build a company with women coaches for girls' teams. We called it Kick Start Soccer Academy. It seemed a simple enough idea but it didn't turn out that way. When we went for our coaching licenses, we were surprised to be the only women in the classes and by the condescending attitudes toward us. In the on-field instructional sections it was always a surprise when we executed the skills perfectly. Even after we got our licenses, it wasn't all smooth sailing. In the beginning, we had a hard time finding enough young women to coach, so Teresa and I had to do all the on-field training (rather than managing coaches, as we'd expected). My mother-in-law (Teresa's mother) could only babysit so much, and finding and paying good babysitters was an additional struggle. We had a hard time breaking into local clubs because existing coaches kept maneuvering to keep us out. Local soccer club administrators didn't seem to value our opinion or experience and, to top it all, my daughter didn't really want my opinion either.

———

In 2008, Armando and I were living in a neighborhood in northeastern Queens called Douglaston that had a good public elementary school and an easy train journey to Manhattan. One day, one of my new friends from the neighborhood, Melanie, found out that we were a big family of soccer fanatics.

"Did you know Pelé's daughter, Kely, lives over your back fence?" she asked.

I did not know that Pelé's daughter lived over my back fence. If I had known Pelé's daughter lived over my back fence, I would have spent more time peering over that fence. And that is exactly what I started doing. I imagined one day bumping into Pelé in his pajamas as he picked up his daughter's morning paper. But I never saw Pelé or his daughter at all, and a year later we sold that house and moved farther out on Long Island. I figured I'd missed my chance to meet Pelé's family, and I resigned myself to the fact that Pelé's magic would always be, for me, locked in the epic movie *Escape to Victory* that I had seen as a kid.

Around this time, Madi was old enough to start playing soccer. Armando and I, his dad, his siblings—we all couldn't wait for her to play.

As a first-time mom, I was surprised when she started asserting her personality so vehemently and didn't always agree with me. I was surprised that she didn't like to be told what to do, and when she didn't like the clothes from the girl section of the store. When she was about ten, I took a break from offering her my opinion on things because it seemed a reflex that she would simply choose the opposite. One day she and I were arguing over what she was going to wear to a family wedding and Armando stopped me.

"I don't know why you don't see it," he said. "She's just like you."

He was right. It was so obvious. She was a lot like me when I was her age. She dressed like her brothers, hung out with them and their friends, and wanted to play football. She wanted to make every decision on her own and to make her own mistakes. I was a little bit proud but I also felt for her. It hadn't been easy for me to be different from the other girls. And I hoped she wasn't going to be like me and waste years not heeding good advice.

I was coming up for air after my first decade of motherhood. I'd found new moms' groups at each place we'd lived who made me feel like my crazy wasn't alone. I adored my kids beyond measure, but raising them was the hardest thing I'd ever done. It was like getting my butt kicked up and down the field all the time by minions who wouldn't listen. So many opinions and so much mess. Once the younger two were expressing their personalities I really stopped taking it personally that my daughter was so unenthusiastic about my opinion. They were who they were. It also made me think about my sister. Maybe we were that way too. Maybe all the theories about how to help us individualize were a complete waste of time.

My guilty pleasure was sitting down at my laptop. I wasn't getting through my list of things to do: cooking, cleaning, laundry, school obligations, community events, the kids' schedules. Getting dinner on the table, which I wasn't getting any better at, still seemed to always take me half the day, and more often than not was a complete waste because the entire family including Armando looked at it like I had put a plate of tarantulas in front of them. I couldn't compete with his mom's homemade Sicilian lobster sauce. Researching the amazing women in sports who came before me was the perfect escape.

I found myself looking up Billie and Donna and trying to find more of the women pioneers in sports. I found lists of their achievements but I kept looking for their *stories*. I found some of what I was yearning for in books, and I started to feel in my heart the connection I'd been needing to find, the impact that they'd had on my life. I found stories of how the first female athletes had persevered to play the games they loved and I noticed that, in doing so, these women were always on the front line of the larger movement in their community toward girls being allowed to do all the same things as boys. They were stories about women who defied stigmas to participate in male-dominated realms, breaking down one barrier at a time. Each book led me to more books, and the more I read the more questions I had.

I'd never been what I would call an avid reader. I was surprised that the books were stacking up next to my bed. I found the stories about Title IX and the women and men who conceived the law—from all different walks of life and for all different reasons—really moving. They stuck with me; I thought about the special combination of traits these people had—the historical awareness, the moral compass, incredible confidence and courage, the willingness to take the backlash—as I went about the rest of my day.

One of these people was Birch Bayh whose father, the superintendent of physical education of Washington DC, had an opportunity to testify before Congress when Birch was a young boy. The father told his son that he was going to testify: "There's going to be a day when we need to appropriate money for girls' physical education, and if they ask why, I'm going to say that little girls need strong bodies to carry strong minds around in, just like the little boys do."

When he was a young man, Birch fell in love with a farmer's daughter from Oklahoma named Marvella Hern when she beat him in a speech contest. She was a straight-A student and the first female president of her high school's student body. They were both devastated when her application to her dream college, the University of Virginia, was returned to her with the response: "Women need not apply."

Just over a dozen years later, then Senator Birch Bayh of Indiana, had picked up the work started during the 1920s to pass an Equal Rights Amendment to protect women's rights as equal citizens in the American constitution but the opposition was stalling the amendments ratification. There were thousands of state and federal laws that discriminated against women. There were laws that said the husband is the master of the community and the wife is obliged to obey. Marital rape was not prosecuted. Employers in most states could legally fire a woman for being pregnant. Banks could legally require a woman to have her husband co-sign any credit she applied for. Passing an Equal Rights Amendment was going to be a long process.

Seeing it another way, Senator Bayh reused a section of the Civil Rights Act of 1964 that prohibited discrimination on the basis of race, color or national origin in programs or activities that receive federal funds to include the one group that had been left out. He wrote the words: "No person in the United States shall, on the basis of sex, be excluded from participation in, be denied the benefits of, or be subjected to discrimination under any education program or activity receiving Federal financial assistance." He added the sentence to a set of amendments of a federal law called the Higher Education Act of 1965. It became known as Title IX of the Education Amendments of 1972, or just Title IX. It wasn't the Equal Rights Amendment that he knew women deserved (and is yet to be ratified) but at least women would no longer be denied access to education programs.

Senator Bayh found strong allies. I was drawn deeper than ever into history, another subject in school that I'd dismissed early on as unimportant and boring. I realized I could not have been more wrong as their stories came alive to me. They were all stories of heartbreak, finding out it was perfectly legal in the United States to discriminate against girls. Each of their stories was equally compelling, like Representative Edith Green from Oregon, the seventeenth woman elected to the US House of Representatives, who noticed there were federal programs designed to keep underprivileged boys in school but not underprivileged girls. And Patsy Mink from Hawaii, who was denied entrance to every medical school she applied to because she was a woman, before she became the first Asian-American woman elected to the US House of Representatives.

And Bernice Sandler, who was repeatedly denied a professorship at the University of Maryland despite her irrefutable qualifications and found a legal precedent to file 269 complaints against colleges and universities that discriminated against women. And Billie Jean King, who focused her efforts at the time on helping pass Title IX, including testifying in the Title IX hearings.

But the work wasn't over once the law was passed. Immediately, complaints were filed and hostility began as the law's impact on athletic programs in schools became clear. There was fierce opposition, particularly trying to remove big-budget sports like men's football from being included in Title IX compliance calculations. The National Collegiate Athletics Association (NCAA) said the law was going to be the end of college sports and so it filed a lawsuit. In response, a coalition of activists began protecting the integrity of the law and has been actively doing so for half a century. If it weren't for their vigilance and perseverance, the law would no longer apply to sports and the sporting landscape in the United States would not have changed.

I had directly and profoundly benefited from a single, thirty-seven-word sentence. It gave me my acceptance into college and it gave me soccer; and those two things were the foundation of my entire life. Absolutely everything. And I'd never even known. Title IX had run in the background of my life, unlocking doors that would have been closed to me otherwise. The legislation's original intent was to end gender discrimination in the US education system. The debate about whether or not to include sports programs—and, if so, which ones—continued to be an epic battle of astonishing proportions. The NCAA and sports directors across the country did not appreciate being told to redistribute their budgets, but the law began to even out the imbalance, revolutionizing the American youth sports system and giving millions of girls the opportunity to play sports.

I asked everyone I knew about the failed Equal Rights Amendment as well as Title IX: people older than me, who might have remembered some of the events first hand, like my parents and in-laws; people my own age, who might have understood the history better than me, like Armando's colleagues at work, and the parents of our children's friends. No one knew very much about either.

I couldn't help re-examining my experiences and placing them in the greater historical context I was just beginning to understand. Some disappointment came along with lifting the curtain. For instance, I'll never forget my first NCAA tournament game with the Harvard women's soccer team. Finding out we'd been selected (after losing the Ivy League title to Brown in my junior year) was electrifying, by far the most exciting moment of my life up to that point. I loved the way it sounded when people said we'd made it to "the Big Dance." We were special, accomplished and, most importantly, recognized on a national level with the biggest teams in the country—men and women—for the first time. That's how I felt. But the reality was different.

In the early days of women's college sports in the United States, the NCAA didn't care to include women. Instead, women's teams created their own separate organization called the Association for Intercollegiate Athletics for Women (AIAW), which was founded in 1971 to administer national championships for women's collegiate teams. The AIAW grew to over 800 members and began to make money from television rights for their women's basketball championships. When Title IX was passed and the NCAA realized that colleges were now going to be forced to invest in women's sports, they decided they needed to take control of the women's championships—and they wrested control of the women's national championships away from the AIAW. The AIAW fought to keep control, even filing an antitrust lawsuit against the NCAA, but the NCAA made it free for colleges to add their women's teams into their organization, and offered other benefits that the AIAW couldn't afford. Schools switched to the NCAA and the AIAW was forced to fold.

The NCAA wasn't what I had imagined.

I was also stunned to find out that during the years I played against Brown at Harvard, young women on the Brown gymnastics and volleyball teams—athletes just like me—had the wherewithal and courage to file a Title IX lawsuit against their university's sports department for being in violation of Title IX when their funding was cut. The university argued that they had one of the best programs for women, which was true, but overall funding and support of women and men was not equitable. The young woman who initiated the case, Amy Cohen, was the cocaptain of the gymnastics team and had graduated (in 1992, the year I arrived at Harvard) but she still carried on with the case—not for herself, but for everyone who came after her. The case went all the way to the US Supreme Court, where Brown's appeal was denied, and in 1997 (the year after I graduated) the university was forced to give varsity status and funding to several women's teams. There are so many more stories like this one spanning the breadth of years since 1972, such as the Yale heavyweight rowing crew team's dramatic Title IX protest in 1976, walking into the sports director's office and stripping to reveal "Title IX" written in marker pen on their chests and backs, all the way up to Eastern Michigan State's softball and tennis teams being reinstated in the autumn of 2019.

———

While I was researching the history of women's sports, I was living my family's own, very sport-centric present. The three kids each had at least one training session a day. They were playing soccer and lacrosse all year, and had various other sports' seasons and training to fit in. The carpool situation was like a house of cards. Luckily Armando's parents provided shuttling and amazing sideline support to fill in the gaps, especially on weekends when we ran from field to field, hoping we had the right kit and equipment.

The world of youth sports my kids were making their way in was different to the one I had experienced. It's not as easy now to take the kids to the school field for a kick-about on a Saturday morning like my dad had done with us; the fields are busier and have strict rules about permits. Each sport comes with expenses for the clubs, the fields the gyms, the coaches, the kit, three kinds of shoes for different surfaces, cold-weather gear, team backpacks, team sweatshirts, travel and camps. The kids tried out each year from eight years old, being divided into A, B, C and D teams, which caused a lot of stress and tears. I told myself that of course everything was going to be expensive and competitive; this was New York, not a place like Oslo, where having fun and participation are the priority and leagues don't keep score until the kids are about thirteen years old. My kids and I would just have to toughen up. Besides, my daughter had almost all the same opportunities my sons did, so could I complain? If I said that youth sports should be about the fun and the lessons, would anyone hear me? Not when college scholarships and admissions advantages and the business of soccer are more important.

The atmosphere at the games wasn't that different to when I was a kid, though, and I soon realized my dad wasn't the only yeller. The only yelling I do on a sideline is cheering, but when I coached my daughter's team I once put my body between a screaming parent and a referee because I could remember—viscerally—how powerless I felt watching my father scream at refs all over Southern California.

———

Over the years, Stauffy had done a great job of getting many of our Harvard Women's Soccer alumnae connected by email, spanning the generations of teams from the late eighties to current players. In 2008, I created a private Facebook group for our alumnae. I thought the space might be like a virtual locker room, allowing us to talk to each other as often as we wanted. I also created a public Facebook group so we could share updates with friends and family.

At a team dinner at Stauffy's house (she pulled the most amazing dinners together for the current team and local alumnae whenever the team was in New York to play Columbia) I asked the coaches and team if anyone might want to start an official Twitter account for the team. I was new to Twitter but it seemed like it had caught on and it might be an easy way to share fun bits of information about the program with the alumnae community and the wider world. I had initially been using Twitter to follow pop culture news, but was increasingly using it to follow women's sports news. I followed people like Shek Borkowski, the coach of the Haitian women's national team.

One day, Shek tweeted a plea for help. I sent a direct message to him, introducing myself and asking what kind of help was needed. I clicked to send the message into the Twittersphere and went back to fighting over vegetables with my three young rug rats and cleaning up the never-ending mess that was our house.

His response came back in minutes: "Susie, thank you for your offer of help. We are looking for thirty small sports bras and twenty-five pairs of cleats."

A rush of energy picked me up. *That I could do!* I typed my answer at superspeed, my mind already planning: "I will get started and get them to you asap. Where should I ship it?"

We went back and forth several more times within thirty minutes of my seeing his tweet. He explained more about their situation, saying: "We have about ninety girls at the national training center, aged twelve to seventeen. They share forty or fifty pairs of cleats and none of them have sports bras."

His message hit me hard. I had never had to worry about equipment. In high school, when our school didn't provide us with kit, we went out and bought what we needed. And this was Haiti's national team. Imagine what their youth sports were like. I knew my teammates would feel the same way I was feeling. We had to help them. I posted a copy of Shek's tweet to our alumnae Facebook page and the responses started to come in instantly.

In a longer email, Shek sent us a thank-you and told me more about the girls:

Susie,

Thank you so very much for your support of Haiti women's soccer programs!

Your generous help is greatly, GREATLY appreciated!

We have a total of about ninety girls/women in our Under-15, Under-17, Under-20 and senior teams. We have great raw talent, which can become some of the finest female players in the world if it is nourished. What we lack is the resources required for development, and because of it Haiti and rest of the Caribbean countries are getting further behind the US, Canada and Mexico in our region.

In Haiti soccer exists in its purest form. The players train and play with joy in their hearts and smiles on their faces. They are innocent about the state of the women's game and believe they can conquer the world. They have no idea about our lack of resources, and sharing forty or fifty pairs of shoes among ninety players is normal—they don't know any better. The young ones don't even know that sports bras exist.

In Haiti, the women's program is dead last on the list of priorities for the Haitian Football Federation. For the most part our players wear old adult male kit. It doesn't faze them; that's how things are and they are content. After coaching in the US and Russia, I am trying in a small way to improve their conditions, and help to develop Haiti women's soccer into potential World Cup qualifier. I know it's a long shot but anything is possible.

Thank you again,

Shek

Within a week, my team and I had arranged to send them the cleats they asked for. And my cocaptain, Noonan, worked with New Balance who generously donated a shipment of sports bras.

To thank us, Shek sent us photos of the girls holding their new gear with handmade signs that said: "Merci Harvard!" It wasn't a large-scale operation—we'd been able to arrange it all online in a matter of days, and they needed so much more—but I felt for the first time that my teammates and I could do something more for young women around the world who wanted to play and for the game that had given so much to us.

In 2013 my cousin Mary Osborne, a professional surfer, told me she was going to be honored by the Women's Sports Foundation, which was founded in 1974—the year I was born—to expand access to sports for girls and to protect Title IX. She invited me to be her plus-one at the organization's annual gala award ceremony called the WSF Annual Salute, where she was being honored for being the first woman to surf the famous wave known as the Silver Dragon on China's Qiantang River, the world's largest and fastest tidal-bore.

That night changed my life. I got to be Mary's sidekick and watch her get glammed up with the glam squad alongside summer and winter Olympians and the biggest names in women's professional sports. We rode in the elevator with Jen Welter, the first female coach in the National Football League, and chatted in the lobby with Sam Gordon, the thirteen-year-old female American football phenomenon. I proudly held Mary's clutch bag as she walked the red carpet and talked to the press. But the event was more than entertaining. At the time, I didn't know very much about the WSF except that it had been founded by Billie Jean King and Donna de Varona and that Foudy was one of its past presidents. But listening to Mary talk about the organization and what it meant to her made me appreciate more the role it had played in women's sporting history.

The event also gave me a chance to reconnect with Julie Foudy in person. Mary knew Foudy was my hero and so she dragged me over to reintroduce us. As one of the hosts, Foudy presented awards to the impressive athletes from that year's biggest sports events, including basketball, soccer, softball, ice skating, hockey, tennis, swimming, motocross, BMX biking, skateboarding, snowboarding, skiing and para-sports.

I knew Foudy had relied on King's advice when the US women's national soccer team had started to negotiate for equitable treatment and pay leading up to the 1996 Olympics and again before the 1999 FIFA Women's World Cup. I also knew that WSF cofounder, the Olympic swimmer Donna de Varona, had been the fearless chair of the 1999 Women's World Cup organizing committee, pushing with conviction for the biggest stadiums in the country. But I hadn't known that Billie and Donna had created WSF to unite female Olympians with professional female athletes in all sports and to build an alliance to protect Title IX (which, at the time, was less than two years old and under heavy attack).

One way the foundation has defended the law was through science.

The data WSF has compiled shows the importance of sports for girls. The benefits extend far beyond fields and tracks and courts. Girls who participate in sport are more content with their lives than girls who do not. They have improved cardiovascular fitness and muscle strength. They have higher levels of self-esteem and lower levels of depression and suicide. They are less likely to engage in risky behaviors like alcohol and drug use, and are half as likely to have an unplanned pregnancy. Female high school athletes are 40 percent more likely to graduate from college than girls who don't play sports. An amazing 94 percent of females who rise to the executive level in their careers played sports growing up. Female athletes are more likely to be civically engaged, be comfortable speaking in public, follow the news and, interestingly, engage in a boycott.

I felt like a wandering soldier who had stumbled upon a uniformed and organized brigade of allies. I felt—even more strongly than I had before—a responsibility to get more involved.

Not long after the foundation's award dinner, I reached out to Nick Gates, a friend from Harvard who had founded Coaches Across Continents, an organization that uses soccer and play to make positive change. He had several years of experience in this world of using sport for social development, so I thought he could give me some idea about the big picture of it all. After catching up about our mutual friends, he began talking excitedly about something called the SDGs, which I'd never heard of. Nick explained that they are the United Nations' Sustainable Development Goals. In 2015, the UN presented a list of seventeen interrelated goals to achieve a better and more sustainable future by 2030. The goals address global issues like poverty, inequality, climate change, health and well-being, peace and justice.

I told him how we had sent the cleats and sports bras to Shek and the players in Haiti and that I was hoping to continue helping more girls somehow. He told me he had recently developed a curriculum called ASK for Choice. The "ASK" stands for attitudes, skills and knowledge—the three things they work on in local communities to help close gender equality gaps. The ASK for Choice curriculum was their strategy for working on the gender equality goal of the SDGs. I hoped to join one of the coaches' programs on site one day, but in the meantime I was proud to join the ASK for Choice advisory team.

Two new worlds were opening up to me: the world of people who use social media for social good and another using sport for social good, also known as sport for development. These worlds fused into a way for me to make the two things I knew something about—soccer and technology—work together to try to help people. Everywhere I turned, I learned something new from someone amazing who was trying to change the world in their own way. And each time someone replied or followed me back on social media, my belief in the positive power of social media grew.

People with years of experience in this sport for development world talked about the power of sport but I wasn't grasping the idea. It sounded good. It was a catchy phrase, but it also felt nebulous. They spoke about the power of all sports and the power of soccer in particular because of its reach. Half of the world's population consider themselves soccer fans —that's 4 billion people. But it wasn't obvious to me what that power actually was. I listened and began to see it. Sports, just like they were in my family, are a shared understanding that have the ability to transcend differences between us and the lines we draw between each other. It's a glue that unites people. And when we are united, we can achieve things that we can't do on our own.

———

When the US women's national team made the final of the 2015 Women's World Cup in Canada, our family and friends gathered to watch it together at a restaurant. The best part was that I didn't even organize it. I was sorry that I wasn't there in Canada to watch the team in person, but I had decided to boycott the tournament and not give FIFA or US Soccer my money because of the way they had handled the turf issue: men's World Cup games had never been—and would never be—played on turf, as turf was a second-rate surface for the game; the women had asked for an equal playing surface and had been denied.

After the US team won—propelled by three goals from Carli Lloyd in the first sixteen minutes, including one from the halfway line—New York saluted them with a ticker-tape parade in Lower Manhattan, the first such parade for a women's sports team in the city's history. My sister-in-law Teresa recruited a big group of us to go and watch the festivities.

I'll never forget the feeling I had on the train into the city that morning. All the kids—boys and girls—were decked out in women's national team gear and were giddy with excitement. And my daughter had come, though I hadn't been sure if she would want to. We went first to watch the broadcast of *Good Morning America*, where we hoped to get a glimpse of some of the players. Teresa knew a producer there and had been told some kids might get picked to ask the players a question, so we talked about what questions the kids would ask if they got the chance. Some of their ideas were serious, such as what it takes to play at the highest level of the game; others were sillier, like whether the women had any superstitions.

Once we got to the show's set in Times Square, it was chaos. So many fans of the team had turned out that I literally lost my children, having entrusted them to Teresa's care. I couldn't see anyone in our group or even the *Good Morning America* set. I was 99 percent sure my kids were safe and 1 percent worried they could have been kidnapped or fallen down a manhole or been run over by a cab. I made myself relax and tried to take in the moment.

When I finally found everyone again, they were even more excited than we all had been on the train. Teresa and the kids *had* got up close, right behind the team. And, as if that wasn't enough, my daughter had been selected to ask a question. I couldn't believe I'd missed it. We rushed to the subway and headed downtown to watch the parade with thousands of other fans of all ages and genders, from all over the country, all dressed in red, white and blue, holding flags and signs. I'd never felt anything like the energy in the crowd that day for a women's sporting event. The feeling was stronger than what I'd felt at WSF's Annual Salute. It was stronger than what I'd experienced at the 1999 Women's World Cup final.

After a bit of googling when I got home, I found the *Good Morning America* segment with the team on YouTube. It was easy to spot Teresa, her children and our friends in the crowd—faces painted and American flags waving—directly behind Abby Wambach, Christie Rampone, Hope Solo, and Julie Ertz. When the camera pulled back, I could see my daughter, Madi, sitting on the concrete with a handful of other kids about her age, wearing the Rampone jersey she had chosen over some of the bigger names like Lloyd, Rapinoe, Morgan, or Wambach, which most of her friends had gone for.

Robin Roberts and George Stephanopoulos turned to the kids. The initial question was a good one: "Who inspired you to first play soccer?"

Ali Krieger answered that her father and brother were her inspiration.

"What are your favorite snack foods?"

Alex Morgan answered that Oreos were a mainstay on the team's snack table.

Then it was my daughter's turn. But there was a problem—her mic wasn't working. On live television. Even watching the clip a day later, I started sweating for her. After she spoke, there was a long, awkward silence. None of the players answered because none of them could hear what she said. But Stephanopoulos jumped in to smooth the situation.

"She said: 'Don't you think you guys should get paid as much as the men?'" he repeated.

The reaction was instantaneous: the team, the crowd and the two hosts roared.

———

Right after that World Cup, I caught up with my friend Melanie in Douglaston. After we filled each other in on our lives and family, I told her about how my book was morphing into a kind of feminist awakening story.

"Why haven't you met Kely yet?" she asked. "This is ridiculous. You're working on the *same thing*."

The next week, Melanie invited us both to dinner.

When I walked up to the table that night, the holy-shit awe I was experiencing was because of who Kely's dad was... but Pelé never even came up in conversation. We had so much to talk about and so many interests in common that, by the time I got up from the table, my awe was for Kely alone.

Soon, I learned about her background in design and photography, her previous work in fashion, and about the film she was working on to raise awareness of the fact that only 1 percent of soccer players in Brazil are girls and women. The sport had actually been illegal for girls between 1941 and 1979 because the government at the time thought it wasn't compatible with feminine nature. Even today, Brazilian players are pressured to keep looking feminine to stay on their team, and in 2011 the Santos women's team was asked to produce a calendar featuring them in bikinis.

I told her about my own work, how as the books I was reading were piling up I felt a little like Rocky Balboa in one of his epic get-ready-for-the-big-fight montages. I told her that women in Germany and England had also been banned from the game for almost exactly the same time period as Brazilian women and it seemed that the reason in England was because at the time the popularity of the women's teams (like Dick, Kerr Ladies) was seen as a threat to the sustainability of the men's game. I also told her how I'd recently connected on Twitter with two amazing women, an American woman named Kelly Lindsey who was the head coach of the Afghanistan women's national team, and a woman whose real name is closely guarded, known on Twitter as @OpenStadiums, who was leading a protest in Iran against the ban of women as spectators in soccer stadiums.

Our budding friendship was the start of a collaboration that would change my life in unimaginable ways. We began to combine our expertise and share our networks and opportunities. If I was invited to something about the development of the sport, I brought her along—and vice versa. Sometimes we found out we were scheduled for the same events. In 2017, my Coaches Across Continents ASK for Choice team entered a squad at an event called the Global Goals World Cup, a women's soccer tournament that keeps track of teams' records on the field but also awards points for activism in pursuit of the SDGs off the field. The championship takes place during the UN General Assembly in New York every year, and in 2017 Kely was there as one of the ambassadors for the Global Goals World Cup.

I tore my MCL in the first game. I got overexcited to be back in the game and I fell back into the win-at-all-costs, reckless-abandon playing style that I'd learned to please my dad. It was a brutal lesson but a good one; I had to take care of myself, put my health first—not just in the game but in my whole life. But the activism I was witnessing was inspiring, and the pain was worth the partnerships I was forming. After all, you can't make progress alone.

One of the connections we made that day was with Mara Gubuan, founder of an organization named the Equality League. We faced Mara's team, the Equality Enforcers, in our last game. Mara says she started Equality League to advance women's rights by removing institutional and cultural barriers to sport, a mission we shared but hadn't articulated so elegantly. Equality League improves access, equality and safety in sport for female athletes worldwide. They created the #NoBan4Women petition to support Iranian activists including the group I'd connected to @OpenStadiums. Equality League pressured FIFA to force the Iranian Football Federation to stop the forty-year-old stadium ban on women as spectators of men's soccer matches. In October 2019 the ban was lifted, although not completely or permanently. On the topic of equality, they are supporting the USWNT and women in soccer worldwide to pursue equal pay, prize money, investments, protection, representation and opportunities. Finally, on safety, Equality League leads and supports campaigns to implement and uphold policy in sports organizations like USA Gymnastics and FIFA. They supported films, books, articles and presentations for victims to tell their stories. In a short time, they have affected positive social change. I could not be in greater awe of them.

Around this time, Armando knew that I was working on something, but I still didn't have anything tangible to show for my efforts, so he started talking about me getting a real job.

Putting a résumé together after being at home to raise our kids for thirteen years was like streaking naked through Harvard Square without my teammates. In other words: not fun and very scary. But I pieced it together, suspending the way I had been taught to think about value. I added my book, the soccer academy that I cofounded with Teresa, my work with Coaches Across Continents, my support of the Haitian women's team, and a couple of investments that I'd made (one a documentary that ended up being nominated for an Academy Award, and another a female-founded start-up that was designing STEM toys for girls and that was acquired by a large international toy company).

Feeling confident and excited, I applied for an internship at Major League Soccer. I was rejected. My contact said I was overqualified, but I'm sure he was also considering how awkward it would be to have a forty-year-old mom as an intern. I didn't care about who or what was awkward. I wanted a chance to get my foot in the door for a real soccer job.

In the meantime, friends of mine at ESPN invited me to an event called the espnW Summit, a three-day networking and wellness conference at a hotel overlooking the ocean in Newport Beach, California, where you got to work out every morning and wear athleisure clothing the whole time. My injured knee put a damper on my activities but the trip was worthwhile anyway: I got to see my family; I got to see Foudy; I got to meet people like Kate Fagan, Sarah Spain, Laura Gentile, Alison Overholt and Becca Roux.

The most important moment of the weekend came when a woman I'd just met said to me: "Stop saying you're home with your kids and *kind of* writing a book. Just say: 'I'm writing a book.'"

I still felt like I didn't belong a lot, but whenever I did have the courage to put myself out there, the experience was always worth it so it was getting easier. I felt like I was getting closer to finding what I was looking for, but I still needed a team.

Building on my momentum, I took the train up to Boston for a conference on Gender, Sports and the Media at the Radcliffe Institute for Advanced Study. At night, in my hotel room by myself, I felt very alone. I missed my home, Armando and the kids. But during the day, I felt like I was right where I was supposed to be.

I learned that only 4 percent of sports media in the United States is devoted to women's sports. And that number was not rising. The message that number sends is that no one cares about women's sports, but I knew that wasn't true. I knew there were millions of girls around the world who grew up playing or appreciating sports. Of course they wanted to see people who looked like them on television, in the newspapers and on social media. Breaking down historic barriers seems impossible but it's not. Donna de Varona and the 99ers proved that there is a global television audience for women's soccer and inspired the current generation of players to play. The Portland Thorns in the NWSL have a thriving culture and fan club, the Rose City Riveters, averaging over 20,000 fans per game.

I felt more strongly than ever that there was a place for my book, that it could play a small part in filling a very large hole, so I tried to speed up my work on it. It had grown from a fun and hopefully meaningful story about a women's sports team, into a broader one including the complex history of Title IX, the dearth of laws like Title IX outside the United States protecting investment in girls access to sports, and the status of women's rights around the world. I wanted to wrap it all up but the scope was still growing faster than I could keep up with. It had become so heavy —all the reality—the hard truths in the history of girls and women.

Realizing how sheltered I'd been, I was hearing gut-wrenching stories for the first time of terrible things that happened to girls around the world. Stories of feet-binding, restrictive clothing, restricted movement, restricted rights, restricted education, restricted opportunities, restricted access. Disappointment, abandonment and murder of female babies at birth. Girls sold or bartered away to strangers. Child brides. Arranged marriages. Concurrent wives. Slavery. Physical, emotional and financial fear. Sexual abuse. Female circumcision. Gaslighting. Backlash. Powerlessness.

So much history. So many issues. So much to change. It was overwhelming.

———

In June 2019, my daughter was grinding out her last few days of eighth grade and about to compete in a qualifying tournament for a national competition with her lacrosse team. The tournament was important enough that the team was taking a Friday off from school to attend.

That morning, when we woke up, she and I both had a fever, but she said right away: "Mom, we're going."

Armando, who normally pushes our children to live up to their commitments with no excuses, encouraged her to sit the weekend out.

"I know you want to go," he said. "But you don't want to go and not play your best."

The implication was clear. If she wasn't going to be able to help her team, she should stay home. But it was a big moment in her mind. Winning meant a chance to play in the national tournament. I tried to reason with her: she was only in the eighth grade; it was just one tournament; we were both sick. But I could feel how much she wanted to play and, what's more, I could remember how I had always wanted to play too, no matter what.

"Let's take a minute," I said. "Go shower, and then we'll decide."

Ten minutes later, she was standing at my bedside, dressed in her kit, wet hair wrapped in a towel.

"Let's go," she said. "I'll be ready in ten minutes."

I definitely wanted to go back to sleep. I knew there was a chance I was going to regret letting my daughter play with a fever. But what did I expect? She was my daughter. She was my father's granddaughter. I knew I needed to let her be a warrior.

"All right," I said.

As I was walking back to my bedroom to get dressed, I heard her yell-whisper to herself: "LET'S GOOOO!"

She played all three games of the tournament. I thought I saw her start to struggle a little bit during the second match but she recovered and then had one of the best games of her life in the third. I won't pretend I wasn't grateful to climb into my bed when we got home, but I was so happy we had made the trip.

The following autumn, she was in her first year of high school. One morning after Armando left for work but before the kids were awake, I found a sticky note on her social studies textbook on top of my laptop where I leave it each night.

The note said: "Hi Mom, look at pages 36–38 in my traditions/encounters textbook for evidence of how patriarchies began if you need more for your book."

Smiling, I walked into the kitchen to turn on the lights and start the morning routine of breakfasts, snacks, lunches. Her leaving that book there for me with the little note on it was the best present anyone had ever given me. She was getting it. And she was getting me.

My heart was full of relief. She knows what I didn't know. She appreciates what I didn't appreciate. She knows that the freedoms and opportunities that we have cannot be taken for granted. She knows that courageous people fought long and hard to get us to this point and that we still have a long way to go before full equality. And now she and I are continuing to learn together. But I'd been wondering lately about my boys —did they know too? I wasn't so sure.

Starting with the little things in our daily lives as they were growing up, I had always made a point of nagging my kids equally. No one sat down after dinner until everything was clean, and everyone helped with the laundry. I had been trying to teach them that all humans are equal. But the boys weren't noticing things that weren't equal and asking me about them; instead, my feminism had become kind of a joke. My youngest son would point and laugh and say in a mocking tone: "Hey guys, look! Mom will like that because it says 'Equal Pay.'" So I had to worry about how well I was doing with my boys.

One Sunday afternoon, I was sitting in my makeshift office (me on a couch with a messy pile of books), working on my laptop while my eighth-grade son played video games in the same room. I had kind of invaded what was once primarily his post-homework relaxation zone. Since I'd been parking myself in that room, we spoke sometimes, but most of the time we both went about our business.

"So what's your book about?" he asked.

I looked at him and laughed and then went back to my work. But I noticed he hadn't gone back to his video game and that he was looking at me, waiting for me to speak. So I looked back at him and panicked a little bit about how to explain it to him.

"Well, it's the story of how I grew up but it's really about more than just my life," I started. Then I had nothing to go next. I waited for the next thought but it didn't come. How could I sum it all up for him? I felt a lot of pressure to get my explanation right for him and keep his attention. After a long pause, I finally gave it a try.

"OK, so I think you know that when I was young I was encouraged to be an athlete and a student, right? My parents wanted me to be a soccer player and they also expected me to do well in school. When I got older I learned that girls didn't always have those opportunities the way boys did. And then I learned that there are millions of girls around the world who still don't have those opportunities. I started to learn about all the people who stood up and fought to give me the same opportunities that boys had even though a lot of people around them, close to them, doubted them and tried to get them to stop. I was a little upset at myself that I didn't know the stories because I felt like I hadn't been paying attention, but I realized that it wasn't just me not paying attention when I was young, it was also that a lot of the stories are hard to find. They weren't taught in school and they weren't on television or in movies or newspapers or the places we usually hear stories."

I paused for a second to take in his reaction and see if I should keep going.

He took a breath and said: "So your book, it's really not history. Like *his* story. It's really herstory. Like *her* story. Right, Mom?"

Stunned, I just looked at him: "Yes. Yes, that's right."

I took a moment to savor the feeling.

———

Kely's research, like mine, had widened its focus. The scope of her film was also expanding. The barriers for women to play soccer in Brazil were what had opened her eyes but, like me, she quickly saw that the barriers for women are everywhere.

In late 2017, she asked if I could put my job search on hold, saying: "I might have something for you in January."

"Sure," I said, not having any idea what that might mean.

I knew her documentary had begun as an investigation into the women's team at Santos—the famous soccer club where her father had played—and the city where she was born, as seen through the eyes of a young Brazilian soccer player named Lais Araujo who hoped soccer would help lift her family out of poverty the way it had done for so many male players. But I had no idea how far the film would expand or how I might play a role.

On January 2, shortly after I had put my kids on the school bus, I got a text from Kely: "Hey, do you have a minute? Can I call you?"

"Sure!" I texted back.

When we spoke, her words floored me: "Do you want to be a producer on my movie?"

"Oh my god! Yes!" I said, so happy. Everything that had previously seemed scattershot—all my non-real jobs—suddenly came together. And, just like that, I got the coolest job in the world.

Kely's documentary, *Warriors of a Beautiful Game*, was a perfect fit for me. In our own way, we were both trying to understand the struggle for gender equality through the lens of sport. Like my book, it was a story about a female athlete (although, let's be clear, Lais's soccer career has far outpaced my own), the kind of story I'd been looking for since having my daughter. One that would help people see that making the world better for women matters. From the first moment she mentioned it to me, I knew Kely's film was going to make a big impact.

Armando's family, my family back in California and my teammates rallied to support us. My mom and dad, Katie and my brother Tom had always been supporters of my writing, reading whatever I sent them as often as I asked, as had my Harvard teammates. It made the distance between us feel smaller. However, there were many times when I sent one of them something to read with a pit in my stomach, anxious about their reaction. Digging into uncomfortable or shameful memories was difficult, and then sharing them was terrifying. But time after time, talking was healing. The process was healing. And being involved in this film with Kely was an incredibly uplifting next step.

Our little production began our initial outreach for fundraising, and my parents, Katie, Tom, my teammates and friends all immediately supported us and helped get us going. One of my first contributions to the film was good, old-fashioned Rolodexing. First, I introduced Kely to Foudy, who I had kept in touch with since reconnecting at WSF's Annual Salute, and Foudy agreed to join as our executive producer. This development in my life was mind-blowing. Foudy was my childhood hero; I had looked up to her for thirty years. Now we were working together. Over the years, seeing other heroes and role models fall from grace, it wasn't lost on me how amazing it was to have a hero stay so solidly on their pedestal and keep being a leader in each phase of life.

Next, I connected Kely—my new teammate—to my Harvard team. The new coach of the Harvard women's team—an all-around great guy named Chris Hamblin—had forwarded me an email about a conference at Harvard called Participation, Inclusion and Social Responsibility in Global Sports. I contacted the organizers who invited Kely and I to sit on the panel about gender inclusion.

I didn't actually want to sit on a panel. I'd never been an "expert" before, and the idea scared me to death. Especially a panel at Harvard, where I'd barely raised my hand as a student. I had the same feeling as when I'd agreed to jump out of an airplane (twice). I knew I was going to do it, but if I died suddenly and painlessly before that happened I might be OK with that outcome.

The first day of the conference was focused on the Qatar World Cup, FIFA, the politics of World Cup decisions, back-room dealings, money, and corruption. There were discussions about the ethics of player migration, trafficking, and the big business side of sports.

That night there was a dinner at the university's Loeb House, which had previously been the residence of Harvard presidents. The house was abuzz because executives from Barcelona—one of the best teams in the world and home to the Pelé-like Lionel Messi—had arrived. The club's president, Josep Bartomeu, was the keynote speaker for the night.

Kely and I grabbed a glass of wine from the bar. Before long, Josep Bartomeu walked right up to us with a big smile on his face as I thought to myself: *Holy shit, what is happening?* Determined not to go tongue-tied the way I had in past momentous meetings, I scraped together my most formal introduction: "What an honor to meet you, President Bartomeu. I'm Susie Petruccelli."

Without expecting to, I bowed my head, trying to make the gesture of deference be noticeable but not weird. Smoothness under pressure is not one of my strengths—at least, not since I hung up my cleats—but I sure as hell was going to pretend to be smooth.

"And this is my colleague, Kely Nascimento-DeLuca," I continued.

"Yes. I know who you are," he said. *What the fuck? Did he just say that?* And then, before I could recover, he added: "And I've heard all about your project."

Kely and I looked at each other in disbelief. *He* was excited to talk to *us*. How had he heard about us? Struck by his genuine and friendly demeanor we started babbling away, answering his questions about our project and talking about Barcelona's women's team. He spoke with pride about their star players, including Lieke Martens, a Dutch striker who was the reigning UEFA and FIFA Player of the Year at the time. At the end of the conversation he said: "I think we are going to do great things together." It was an unbelievable moment.

The next day—the day of our panel—brought me back down to earth. I woke up full of anxiety. Still, the high from the previous night did help. I needed to turn a corner on my outlook on public speaking. I was ready. I remembered a quote I'd read from Dr. Colleen Hacker, the sports psychologist of the USWNT. Right before the 1999 Women's World Cup, she told the team: "Butterflies are a great thing. They mean you care. Now just teach them to fly in formation."

Sitting at the front of the room with the amazing women on the panel—including Maya Mendoza-Exstrom, General Counsel of the Seattle Sounders of Major League Soccer, and Rebekah Salwasser, the Executive Director of the Boston Red Sox Foundation of Major League Baseball, and Kely next to me—I decided to hammer a couple of ice axes in and not allow myself to slide down the slippery slope of imposter syndrome. I'd been immersing myself in the topic of gender equality—and, by extension, inclusion—for years by that time. I'd lived through my own instances of gender exclusion and knew that every woman has experienced gender exclusion whether we recognize it or not. By telling our stories, we will recognize those experiences in our own lives. We may have accepted the inequalities in our lives as normal, but that doesn't mean we can't stand up and say that that normal has changed for our daughters and granddaughters and future generations.

Once the panel got going, I settled in. It helped me stay calm to know that if my nerves made me miss a question, I just had to ask to hear it again. And trust that if I spoke from my experience and from my heart, I would be fine. I told myself that everyone in the room was there because they were on our team, and I should not be nervous in a room full of teammates, but I couldn't fool myself. I knew if I misspoke, someone would point it out. I felt so much pressure to speak well and, more than that, the idealistic little girl inside me wanted to reach people's hearts and inspire them to help us. I wanted to be a leader, but the pressure was real and scary and I worried I didn't have the experience or talent or eloquence or charm to manage it.

In that moment, a memory came to my mind. I recalled being at a Women's Sports Foundation event in New York City in honor of the forty-fifth anniversary of Title IX. I remembered the exhilaration I felt when Billie Jean King walked up to the podium, only a stone's throw away from where I was standing. I'll never forget how she explained to all of us in the room the meaning of one of her famous quotations, which is also the title of one of her books: "pressure is a privilege." The meaning of her words finally snapped into all the right places in my soul. This was the moment that I needed to speak those words to myself. This was the moment in which I needed to reframe the pressure I was feeling not as something that had to be managed and overcome, but as a privilege to be grateful for and make the most of. I was blessed to be in such a special position. *I get it Billie,* I thought. *Thank you again for your wisdom.*

Not long after the conference at Harvard, filming for the documentary began. Kely and Justin Noto, the codirector, assembled a small crew—I was part of a crew! Our first trip was to Florida. Arriving at the airport for our early-morning flight and meeting up with Kely and Justin, I felt like I'd had the best night's sleep of my life. It was very early for energetic selfies but I couldn't help myself. I hadn't felt so bright-eyed—like the lights were on again in that unique way—in a very long time.

I'd been home, in my comfortable cave, for a very long time so as the trip continued I oscillated wildly between pure excitement about where my life had taken me and feeling like I would be way more comfortable back in my kitchen, stressing about the day's carpools and what had happened on the playground that day. But this trip was necessary and I knew it. It was necessary to document the story of how Lais had disrupted the status quo to step into a boys' world, the barriers she bulldozed—without compromising her kind and decent nature—in pursuit of her dream and her desperate and honorable goal to provide for her family. So many of my own dreams had come true, but the biggest one we were still pursuing together: the elusive "real job."

We spent the first day of filming following Lais around on the University of Florida campus to set the scene as she was wrapping up her junior year and moving out of her dorm room. On the second day, a new member of our team arrived, a cinematographer named Eric Branco. There was a quiet wisdom about him, the kind of street smarts that I've always loved about native New Yorkers. I could only wager a guess at the things he'd seen. Kely was chasing the truth and beauty of the women's game, and I had a good feeling that Eric was going to catch it for us.

We took the two-hour drive south with Lais to Orlando and filmed her as she started training for the summer with the National Women's Soccer

League's Orlando Pride. It was every young soccer player's dream— to be on the field with a pro team—and with her childhood idol, no less, who also happened to be the best player in the world: the one and only Marta. It took a lot of courage for Lais to get out there and play with the woman voted the world's best player six times, the player Pelé once called "Pelé in a skirt," the fiercest warrior of women's soccer in the world.

We caught their first interactions on the field and the other Orlando Pride superstars, including Alex Morgan, Ali Krieger, Ashlyn Harris, Sydney Leroux, and the other famous Brazilian players like Monica and Camilla. Lais was adorable, completely awestruck to be in the presence of all of those famous players—particularly Marta, of course. After the first training session we giggled with her and hugged her, sharing in the afterglow of her fantasy that had come true.

In order to make all the travel work, I had to face the childcare challenge. The kids were older, the youngest now eight years old, and Madi's health issues had now stabilized. Armando was leaving for work before 6am and returning after 6pm. So if I was going to be away from home, we needed someone in the house on weekdays to get everyone out of bed and on the bus, and everything in between. We needed someone to cover any spontaneous sick days and then someone to manage the driving to and from all the afternoon activities, to oversee homework and to feed everyone dinner. I still had anxiety about how it was going to work but I didn't let it stop me this time.

In the beginning, each time I traveled we had relied heavily on Armando's parents. They had moved into our house to be there around the clock every time I was away, but we were putting too heavy a strain on them. We decided to try the au pair route. It seemed like a cost-effective option for what we needed. We never discussed a real full-time nanny. I was afraid to suggest it because I wasn't bringing in a steady paycheck; my pay was dependent on the completion of the film. I worried that at some point Armando might point out this job wasn't exactly what he'd had in mind.

Our first au pair had a penchant for Facetiming while driving. I helped pay for her to go visit her family for Christmas because she was so homesick, and she never came back, which was probably for the best. Our second au pair was a sweet young girl who was dependable and a very safe driver. It freed me up to finish our travel schedule.

A few weeks after our first trip to Florida, we flew to Brazil. The little soccer nut inside me was bursting with delight when we arrived at our lodging: we were staying in Pelé's apartment, surrounded by his belongings. One of his guitars was in a corner by a window, one of his soccer balls was on the patio on the rooftop deck, a sculpture of two soccer players fighting for a ball was next to the television, a really spooky painting of Jesus Christ hung on the wall over my bed. It was fantastic.

We got to work filming the Santos women's team at their training facility. This would inform the audience (and us!) about what it was like to be a female professional soccer player at one of the wealthiest and most famous soccer clubs in Brazil and the world. Unlike the Santos men's team, which had its own training center with the look, feel, and security of an Olympic Village, the women shared space with the club's all-male youth teams. The women's team was the club's only female team. The women's training fields were totally adequate, with a structure that had changing rooms and toilets inside. The men's training ground was a compound of several buildings and fields, much more impressive and strikingly modern.

We interviewed Emily Lima, the women's coach. We'd been hoping to hear her story not only at Santos but also about how she had been the first female head coach of the Brazilian women's national team and had been recently replaced. When she was fired by the Brazilian socccer federation (known by the acronym CBF), five top players quit the team out of frustration. We also interviewed two veteran players at Santos, both with national team experience. One of them, Rosana, was one of eight members of the national team who had signed an open letter criticizing the federation after Lima's dismissal. The letter read: "We, the players, have invested years of our own lives and all of our energy to build this team and this sport to its strength today. Yet we, and almost all other

Brazilian women, are excluded from the leadership and decision-making for our own team and our own sport."

The most high-profile player to quit, Cristiane, posted a video on YouTube explaining her decision. She spoke for ten minutes about her frustration over Lima's firing, about getting paid $78 per day without a raise for years, with no discussion over image rights and less than $1,000 in salary for an entire Olympic year, about the refusal of the CBF to sell the women's jerseys, about her exhaustion on hearing from the CBF that they only survived because of money from the men's team, about there being no attempt to create a plan for the women's team to become financially independent, about the lack of coaching courses for current and former players or pathways into leadership roles in the federation, and about a total refusal to listen to the players' concerns and requests. She said she had been called annoying for talking too much. She said she was leaving to protect her own health and sanity. Her voice started to crack after almost eight minutes, when she said that other national teams were making progress because they were united in their fight but that she no longer had the strength to fight. No one could possibly doubt that she gave it her all. Seventeen years of her life. Her utter exhaustion emanated from the video, her tears like a plea for forgiveness for needing to give up.

Next, we flew from Sao Paolo to Salvador to film in the favela where Lais got her start in life and in soccer. Her family and neighbors welcomed us with open arms and hearts. During our interview with Dilma Mendes, one of Lais's first coaches and an incredible pioneer woman, I cried. It didn't matter that I couldn't understand the Portuguese she was speaking; when her eyes welled up, so did mine.

We made a second trip to Florida to capture Lais's senior soccer season. We also were very fortunate to get some individual time with Marta. As we were wrapping things up with the interview, she noticed I had been crying when she cried (again, despite the language barrier). She said something to Kely in Portuguese, and they laughed.

"What? What did she say?" I asked, wiping my eyes.

"She said: 'Look! I even made the American cry!'" Kely had to explain it to me. Apparently Brazilians think Americans are unemotional.

We also got to interview Abby Wambach at her house around the time her amazing book, *Wolfpack*, was just coming out. Abby gave us the perspective of the middle generation of the US women's national team and described for us her admiration and appreciation for what the 99ers built for her generation.

We continued to travel and film what was happening with women's soccer in other countries. We embarked on a whirlwind, ten-day trip to film at three clubs across Europe. Traveling with film equipment provides exercise for both the mind and body, and security at airports always comes with surprise pitfalls and delays. But pulling up to each of the giant European soccer clubs and being allowed to see inside was worth any amount of sweat, confiscated tools or threatened fines for a mishandled carnet (like a passport for the cameras and production equipment).

What we found at Manchester City filled us with so much hope for the future of women's soccer. Every person we met—from the administrative offices to the executive suite—genuinely believed in the value of the women's team and understood the importance of equity, where both teams may not be in a position of equality but they both have what they need to succeed. The Manchester City women's program was led by a passionate advocate for the women's game, Gavin Makel. The Etihad Campus was a glorious place. Truly glorious. The women shared the same training facilities and their stadium was connected to the men's stadium by a sleek footbridge.

We then hopped to Paris, where we filmed at Paris Saint Germain. Like every stop, we were there to observe what professional women's soccer looks like, and in Paris the culture and fan base for the women's team at PSG blew us away. So did a former player for both PSG and France, Laure Boulleau, who had moved on to hosting the most popular soccer show in France—remarkable because, while breaking down barriers to play is hard, breaking down barriers in sports media is even harder.

Also in Paris, we got to interview both Neymar and his father about their efforts to have the women's team at Santos reinstated after club officials cut the squad as an unnecessary expense. When Neymar walked into the room I actually found myself breathless. He was captivating. He was taller and more handsome than I'd expected. He told us plainly that he knew the girls who played soccer in the streets from church and school, and that he always respected them equally as athletes.

In Torino in Italy, we talked to members of Juventus's women's team, where female soccer is receiving renewed attention. Like Manchester City, the Juventus women have had a meteoric rise. In 2017–18, the squad won the Scudetto (or the Serie A championship) in their inaugural season with Rita Guarino, a five-time Scudetto and Coppa Italia winner, at the helm as coach. They then followed that up with a second consecutive Scudetto in 2019.

One of the club's players, Eniola Aluko, had stood up to discrimination from her former English national team coach (and was never called back up to the national team despite his dismissal). We listened to her explain her experiences, entranced by her incredible poise and eloquent storytelling.

Our interview with the head of women's soccer at Juventus was a little disheartening. He told us he believes girls in Italy are just not as interested in soccer as boys. That sounded familiar; similar reasoning had come up time and time again in the Title IX court cases I'd been reading about. But the statistics don't back that sentiment. For example, in the US between 1972, when Title IX was passed, and 1991, when FIFA held the first official women's world championship, there was a 17,000 percent increase in girls playing soccer in high school. I remembered my experience when Armando and I had lived in Italy and I'd let myself be intimidated off the soccer field by the local men and boys. I believe there are girls in Italy who would play if they were welcomed onto the field.

In Zanzibar, we were hosted by Fatma, a young women's rights advocate who was helping us connect with local soccer teams. Her reputation as a kind and intelligent leader preceded her. We had heard about her work on behalf of women and children in her community from a few people, including my friend Nick at Coaches Across Continents. In person, she was even more extraordinary—a beautiful soul, just like Lais. She had us over for dinner at her family's house, and it was a feast. We noticed her grandmother was struggling to walk up and down the steps, and Fatma explained that she had chronic joint pain. Her pain was obviously severe. I recognized the look on her face from the worst moments of my injury rehabilitation. Seeing her grandmother in pain because of health issues that are preventable is one of the reasons why Fatma is pushing for change. She is finding a way to work within the boundaries of modesty and respect of her beloved culture to change things for her grandmother, mother and aunts, and future generations facing the risk of hypertension, arthritis and other conditions that are preventable with moderate exercise, starting with allowing girls to play sport in schools.

With Fatma, we also watched and filmed professional women's soccer throughout the island of Zanzibar. Before we arrived I had read articles about the struggles of the women players and had assumed the women were pressured not to play. I knew very little about the local cultural customs—the clothes they wore, what they were called, who wore them or why. The women all seemed to cover their heads in some way and wear long gowns, which I assumed would feel restrictive. We set up our cameras at the side of the field and waited for the women to arrive. They walked up and stepped out of their clothing to reveal shirts, shorts, shinpads and cleats—each with her own choices in terms of modesty, sometimes a tight covering over her hair, a few with long sleeves, others with long pants. They were so casual about it; it seemed no different to the way we changed out of our school uniforms or daily clothes. We all have cultural uniforms of one kind of another. But was this dangerous and risky for a woman who is expected to be in a hijab? Was it illegal under the law or enforced by religion? What does it mean in their lives when they take off the hijab in public?

One afternoon, I had a nice long kick-about with Riziq, one of the players in Zanzibar. During a break in filming, I caught her attention, showed her the ball, putting it on the ground and kicked it to her before breaking away and gesturing for the pass. When she smiled, I knew she had understood, and the game took over. We communicated without language; it didn't matter that she spoke Swahili and I spoke English. We smiled and laughed and shared the game. It was like taking part in a choreographed dance we both knew. That understanding we shared will always be there inside both of us. Our cultures, our religions, our languages, the clothes we wear—all our differences melt away on the field as we unite in the freedom of the game.

In Zanzibar I started to reflect on a pattern. I noticed that each time we were planning to go and film somewhere new I formed an image of what I expected to find there. And each time I was wrong. We had to see it for ourselves. We had to speak to the women there. I'd done the same at other times in my life—I'd formed conclusions about things and people that were later proven wrong. Like my dad, who worked so hard to provide me with what I needed and wanted, driving me to training and games, being totally invested in my life, while I'd so often focused on the negatives and failed to appreciate the positives.

Working on the film was the most intellectually stimulating thing I'd ever done, and feeling so reconnected to the game was filling the void that had opened up in my life after I finished playing, but things were falling out of balance at home. My travel schedule was hard on our kids—their grades were slipping and there were lots of teary phone calls. I'd been loving the work, but the old adage was true: I could only be as happy as my most unhappy kid.

———

In the spring of 2018, I saw a tweet from an organization that I'd been following in the UK called Women in Football, a nonprofit working to support girls and women in all areas of the game. The group was launching what it called the #WhatIf Campaign. The idea was for businesses, celebrities and individuals to make a pledge to help the progress of girls and women in the soccer industry. *Brilliant*, I thought. I watched as the pledges started rolling in. The English Football Association offered a program for future female leaders in the game. A giant HR company offered to support women in their transition to the labor force after

TO NY AND BEYOND

their playing careers. Famous coaches offered to mentor young female coaches. Sky Sports offered internships. Agents and lawyers offered guidance and support. Well-established sports journalists offered mentor-ships to young female journalists. Soccer federations offered tickets for female fans. It went viral.

By chance, one of the first #WhatIf pledges I saw came from Ian Ridley, a writer I was already following because I'd found him in the early phase of writing my book when I was reading as many sports memoirs as I could find. His pledge was: "#WhatIf I mentor a young female football writer." At forty-four, I wasn't really young anymore. I also still didn't really consider myself a soccer writer, or any kind of writer at all. But I replied to his tweet anyway. He responded with a direct message: "Hi Susie, email me if you want to contact me re your sports book."

After exchanging emails, I sent Ian a sample of my book, choosing a section about the final Brown game and the section I'd just written about Madi and the first ticker-tape parade. I was nervous. I sent it with the thought that, if Ian's reaction wasn't positive, I might let the book go. I was grateful for its role in connecting me with Kely, and I thought: *remember that it is OK to quit sometimes.* It was so incredible that Ian had even responded to my tweet—he was a famous writer! *From England!* It could not have been more exciting.

The following day I received his feedback. His words were the best thing I had ever read in my life: "The first thing to say is that there is certainly a book in here and you have a great story to tell."

My mouth dropped open and I gasped, wide-eyed in shock. His email continued, offering suggestions and ideas, and at one point he wrote: "[I] have huge admiration for the struggles of my wife, who is a sports writer and member of Women in Football board in England and has had to endure a lot."

Unbeknownst to me, Ridley's wife was Vikki Orvice. I had heard of her—anyone who followed women's sports writing in England has heard of her. She was a trailblazer in women's sports journalism in England. *Oh my gosh*, I thought. *This is unbelievable.*

Ian explained how to present a proposal to American publishers and wished me well, encouraging me to keep going.

I tried to follow his advice and stick with my writing, but it was hard. When I wasn't traveling for the film, I was trying to be a mom again at home. Something had to give and, with no solid financial prospect in sight, that something was my book. Reluctantly I put it to one side.

Through Twitter, I stayed connected to the #WhatIf conversation. I was saddened to read later that year that Vikki was undergoing treatment for cancer, and in February 2019 she passed away. I was heartbroken for Ian and their family and friends, and for the profound loss for the intrepid group of trailblazing female sports journalists and women in soccer in England.

Ian then set up a prize in Vikki's name, in conjunction with Women in Football as part of the #WhatIf campaign, with a pledge to publish a female author's soccer book. There were twenty entries. I was absolutely amazed and delighted that the judging panel chose my proposal as the winner.

———

In June, our production crew for the film flew to Portland, Oregon. There, we visited Nike's campus, where we had to pinch ourselves when they offered support for our film, and we met Oved Valadez and his innovative team at Industry PDX who became our creative partner. I also went to my first Portland Thorns game and saw how they have turned the dream into a reality. (A Thorns game is a top-notch soccer experience: full stadium, vibrant culture, thriving club.) And to cap the trip, Midge Purce—a recent Harvard women's soccer graduate—scored two goals for the Thorns that day.

My last big trip was to the FIFA Women's World Cup in France. Our friends in women's soccer—like the amazing organization called the Equal Playing Field Initiative, as well as leaders in the women's game including Moya Dodd, Amanda Vandervort, Ashleigh Huffman and espnW—put together an amazing summit in Lyon. They brought together so many people who are working in the movement to grow the women's game and protect players. During the summit I got to participate in the Equal Playing Field Initiative's *third* world-record-breaking soccer match. I'd missed the first two matches—the first at the top of Mount Kilimanjaro and the second at the Dead Sea—but had been able to help with the production of the documentary by a talented young filmmaker named Amirose Eisenbach, which tells the story of the first two expeditions, not only an entertaining group of people but a striking metaphor for how far girls and women will go to play the game they love. That week, I finally met Kelly Lindsey—the coach of the Afghanistan women's national team—and had the incredible honor of meeting Kelly's great supporter, HRH Prince Ali Bin Al-Hussein of Jordan. Together with the organization founded by HRH Prince Ali, AFDP Global, they launched an initiative called #FearlessFootball to support the Afghanistan women's national team and combat abuse, harassment and exploitation in women's soccer worldwide. I also had the pleasure of meeting Bex Smith at the Copa90 Clubhouse in Lyon. Bex is the Global Executive Director of the Women's Game for Copa90, a media company dedicated to celebrating soccer and its fans, and aggressively investing in exciting new media for the women's game.

The masterminds behind the Equal Playing Field Initiative were both working on brilliant next projects. Maggie Murphy was hired as the new General Manager at Lewes FC, the first team in the world to pay its female and male teams equally. And Laura Youngson has invented soccer cleats specifically designed for the ergonomics of women's bodies at her start-up, IDA Sports.

Everywhere I turn, it seems there is progress. Back in Cambridge, Harvard began a crackdown on its final clubs. The university had severed most ties with the groups over their exclusion of women in the eighties, but took additional steps in 2016, withholding leadership roles and resources from any that continued to discriminate. In 2018, the university's nearly 200-year-old theatre group, Hasty Pudding Theatrical, cast its first women performers: six of them, or exactly half the troupe.

When Kely and I went to film Juventus players in Italy, the women's team had never played a game inside the famed Allianz Stadium in Turin.

A few months later, the club defeated Fiorentina there before 39,000 fans, nearly tripling the country's previous attendance record for a women's league game.

FIFA reported that one billion people watched the 2019 Women's World Cup on television, with almost half of that audience coming from Europe, and viewership in South America up 500 percent from the 2015 Women's World Cup. An amazing 82 million people around the world watched the final. On the heels of those record-breaking numbers, new attendance records were set for women's soccer matches around the world, and Sky Blue FC—the perennial underdog of the NWSL—played two games at Red Bull Arena after years of substandard conditions, and has now moved there for the entire 2020 season because of a young and brilliant new general manager named Alyse LaHue.

More exciting news was coming in. Budweiser became the official beer sponsor of the NWSL, and ESPN became the official broadcast partner, including international rights. Mara and Mink and The Equality League's #NoBan4Women campaign got more than 300,000 signatures on their petition and effectively pressured FIFA to intervene with the Iranian Football Federation to begin to allow women into stadiums. The Finnish and New Zealand Football Associations committed to equal pay for its women and men players. In England, Barclays invested £10 million in the FA Women's Super League, and attendance at league games is growing steadily. Women's games in Ecuador and Colombia drew 15,000 and 30,000 fans respectively.

The world record for the biggest attendance at a women's club soccer match is climbing. In 2017 the record was said to be broken in Mexico at a game between Chivas and Pachuca with 32,466 fans. On the heels of that match, the Mexican soccer federation consolidated the first women's professional league in Mexico—Liga MX Femenil—and then, in May 2018, Tigres beat Monterrey on penalties to win the first league title in history in front of what was said to be a new attendance record of 51,211 fans. But it wasn't until six months later that the historic world record (set in December 1920 at a women's club match in England between Dick, Kerr Ladies and St. Helen's Ladies at Everton's Goodison Park with a crowd of 53,000) was finally broken. The record had lasted for almost a hundred years (in large part because the FA banned women's soccer a few months after this match, thwarting the rise of the women's game for fifty years) but on March 3, 2019, Atlético Madrid played FC Barcelona in front of 60,739 spectators at Atlético Madrid's Wanda Metropolitano stadium. Then the Lionesses—England's women's national team—sold out Wembley Stadium for a friendly on November 9, 2019, and the proud crowd erupted in a roar when it was announced they had set a new record for an England Women's international match with 77,768 in attendance despite cold temperatures and driving rain.

According to FIFA, there has been an 85 percent increase in the number of soccer associations around the world running grassroots programs for girls and women in the last five years. Yet there's still a long way to go. Women are still being held back and disrespected, on and off the field.

In 2016, Harvard had to cancel its men's soccer team's season after news broke that its players had been ranking women's team members based on their physical appearance and likely preferred sexual positions.

In Italy, Serie A women's teams' players are still considered amateur athletes, unlike their professional male counterparts, and receive only a per diem instead of a salary, if anything.

Four months before the beginning of the 2018 FIFA Women's World Cup, the US Women's National Team decided they had to do more to fight for equal pay and filed a gender discrimination lawsuit against US Soccer. They filed on International Women's Day.

News was coming in at a steady pace that women's national teams around the world were being vocal and asking for equity from their federations. The women's national teams in Brazil, Argentina, Chile, Puerto Rico, Colombia, Norway, Denmark, Scotland, Australia, Ireland, England, Nigeria, Spain, Trinidad and Tobago and Jamaica and more were standing up and drawing attention to the lack of support from their federations. Each time they speak out, they risk not being invited back to national team training camps. But with the aid of social media and growing connections and support, these women's stories of protest are not as isolated and easily overpowered as they once were. There is a coalition forming that is pulling various groups together, fighting for women's soccer in order to quickly mobilize media support, advocates and lawyers.

There was vast room for improvement in terms of ticketing, marketing and match-day experience at the 2019 Women's World Cup in France. And the gap in prize money between the men's and women's FIFA World Cups is still growing despite the success of the latest women's tournament. For the next set of World Cups, in 2022 and 2023, the *gap* between the prize money for men and women will increase from $370 million to $380 million. That gap exists despite FIFA's $2.7 billion cash reserves and their tax-exempt status, which has as one of its guiding principles to "promote the game of football, protect its integrity and bring the game to all."

One of the most common arguments against equal pay is that women's soccer doesn't bring in the same revenue as men's soccer. At first, this point seems hard to argue. But Becca Roux, the president of the UWSNT Players' Association, succinctly explains why it falls short. The popular metric for revenue is commonly known by the acronym ROI, which stands for Return on Investment. It's a formula that is calculated using two numbers, the value of the investment and the cost of the investment. During a panel at the Equal Playing Field Summit in Lyon, Becca said: "There can't be an R without the I." In other words, there cannot be a return on investment without the investment. Women players are being told they don't deserve more investment because they don't produce as much revenue. But basic economics refutes that argument; the investment must come first.

Looking at it from another angle, national federations around the world, which are nonprofits, are different than for-profit club teams. They are mandated by their own by-laws to invest equally in men and women to grow the game of soccer inclusively. As businesses, club teams don't have that same obligation, although there is certainly a moral argument to be made about valuing public interest over private profits. As veteran soccer journalist Grant Wahl tweeted on September 24, 2019: "FIFA and US Soccer are nonprofit organizations that get huge tax write-offs as a result and are charged with growing the sport for everyone (men & women). Professional teams/leagues are for-profit companies. If you don't understand that fundamental difference, you're nowhere."

There's another analogy that Julie Foudy credits to US women's national team goalie Briana Scurry. Briana said to imagine two gardens side by side. One garden is watered, nurtured and taken care of. The other one is not water or nurtured but told to grow. The watered garden blooms and the other fights for survival. It's hard to build a market when given no water or nourishment.

Long-held perceptions feel impossible to change. Sexism in sports is so normalized that we don't see it. When the kids and I were discussing the Juventus women's record-breaking game in the car one day, Armando interrupted us: "The reason the women never played in the stadium before is because the men's team didn't want them to ruin the grass."

It hurt to hear those words come out of my husband's mouth, the man who had shared Ohiri Field with me at Harvard. I sat dumbfounded in the passenger seat. For years, he had stepped over the piles of my books scattered around our house, he knew I was at events with women's sporting heroes and learning from equality activists, he had swiped through the photos of me with Billie Jean King and Julie Foudy on my phone. He knew how much equality in the game—and in general—means to me, especially for our daughter and her generation. I reminded myself that he had always respected his sisters and Bing and Mink and Stauffy and our team as players, as equals.

But doubt was in the air—my certainty went from black and white to gray. He did respect us equally, didn't he? He did know we are worth the greatest possible playing field just like anyone else? He did know our game isn't as developed economically because we were banned from the game all over the world for most of its developmental years and not because men are actually some kind of "real deal" and women are not? We don't have the same money and power in our game right now because we've been held back over and over again, not because our game is not as entertaining or valuable. Armando had made jokes and laughed with other guys about women's soccer being "underwater soccer," but until that moment I really thought he'd just been joking.

"Do you think that?" I asked him now. "That the women shouldn't be allowed to ruin the grass for the men? You know, the men at Harvard probably said that about our team when we first got started—that the women's team will ruin the grass for the men's team."

Until I said it I had forgotten hearing that. Now I recalled a conversation between two senior players as we were walking back to the dressing room after training one day about how our team had not initially been granted access to Ohiri. That before that it had been reserved for the men. It really does still burn.

He responded: "I'm not saying I agree. I'm saying that's what *they say*."

———

Two days after I got home from Lyon where we watched the US beat the Netherlands in the final, Kely and I were invited to ride in the USWNT's ticker-tape parade through New York City. We were jet-lagged and my luggage was still somewhere in transit, but we wouldn't have missed that parade for the world. Invited as a member of the US Soccer's Supporter's Circle, we rode in one of the open-air buses with other supporters from the very bottom of Manhattan to City Hall.

I wished Madi were with me, the way she had been in 2015. *Good Morning America* had hosted the team again. In 2015, the question of equal pay had been asked by my daughter—a child randomly picked from the crowd—and it wasn't even audible. In 2019, that question was the main focus of the entire segment's discussion. But the question had already been answered, shouted from the nearly 60,000 fans in the Stade de Lyon after the US women won the world championship, by the billion people around the world who watched the tournament, chanted by thousands of adoring fans who listened to Megan Rapinoe deliver remarks at the conclusion of the team's second-ever ticker-tape parade for a women's sports team at New York's City Hall: "Equal Pay! Equal Pay! Equal Pay!"

But Madi wasn't able to be there with me for the parade. In full-circle style, she was with Julie Foudy at one of the Julie Foudy Sports Leadership Academy summer camps. Foudy had sent me a selfie with the two of them from the camp. My hero was officially my daughter's hero. I texted Foudy back that I couldn't wait to give her a big update about the film. So many exciting things had happened since the last time we'd talked. And I sent her a selfie of Kely and I from the top of our bus with the crowded parade route up Broadway in the background.

In that moment, standing there amid all the buzz at the beginning of the parade, the players looking triumphant and cool in their street clothes and sunglasses, and surprisingly well rested for all the hard-earned reveling they had been doing, waving to all the fans from their floats, I felt a double swell of relief: the game was in a good place and so was my daughter. Kely and I had seen for ourselves that there are incredible warriors working around the world to change mindsets and open opportunities for girls and women in all areas of the game and society, and I knew Foudy would teach my daughter what she taught me: to be a leader in her own way; to make a positive impact in the world; to find good role models and listen to their advice; to accept nothing less than equality; and that being a good teammate is what makes you a good human.

The following week, Madi worked at her first job as a coach at my sister-in-law Teresa's camp. Teresa had not only kept the coaching business that we started running despite the challenges but—with very similar instincts to Foudy's about how to positively impact girls' lives—she created a camp called For Girls, By Girls, a soccer-lacrosse-leadership camp. The campers practice the two sports and learn about nutrition, team-building, leadership and maintaining healthy self-esteem. When she couldn't find enough female coaches, she recruited them from local high school and college teams, as she had with my daughter. She trained them, encouraged them and paid them. She also trained them in the administrative and business aspects of her company. She gave them responsibilities, believing in them, and in return they became good coaches and responsible employees; they became leaders. She never stopped working to change mindsets and open opportunities for girls and young women right here in our own community, in our own family. I went all over the world meeting the most amazing warriors of the beautiful game and looking up to my heroes, and I found myself welcomed home with flowers, balloons and proud hugs by one who had been working diligently and effectively as a positive role model for me, my daughter and hundreds of girls in our community the whole time.

———

I had got the tattoo to mark my rock bottom. I had hoped that something as extreme as a tattoo might stop me from sinking any lower. Mink named the tattoo my orbits and it made perfect sense: I'd wanted to stop drifting away to outer orbits where I was making mistakes and feeling shame. I'd wanted desperately to find a new identity since soccer wasn't an option for me any longer. I had set out to find the new me.

As the years passed, the tattoo changed. The orbits didn't looked like orbits; there was no pale skin between them anymore. People started asking me if it was a birthmark. I joked that I wished I had been born with it—and the humility that it came with. The cycles of personal growth continued for me. I would reach a new plateau of understanding, a new core, and then the cycle would start over again. That has been one of the most beautiful parts of my journey and has helped me to see the tattoo differently.

The ink of the tattoo naturally traveled from cell to cell over time and began to fill in the spaces between the rings. It felt like my body was demonstrating to me how to accept my whole self—wherever I was, not a better, future version. I felt a new peacefulness when I stopped searching for some new identity. Finally I understood that my identity was never one single orbit—being a twin, a soccer player, a victim, a wife, a mom, a programmer, a writer, a producer. My identity was always with me. I was born with it. It is the whole energy that I bring to the world.

My dad raised me to be a warrior on the field, which left some scars, but my journey led me here, unfazed by a ball in the face or getting knocked down, knowing the value of hard work and perseverance, more awake, working on myself, educating myself, serving the game, honoring teammates and role models, trying to give back, trying to ensure that all girls have the opportunities and joys that I was so blessed with through the game, trying to raise my own children to be warriors for the many things they will feel in their hearts like I feel this one.

But most of all, I don't want any little girl to be alone when she experiences inequality for the first time. I want to be there letting her know that there is a massive, growing army fighting to make things equal for her before she grows up. This is our responsibility.

ABOUT THE
VIKKI ORVICE PRIZE

The email came out of the blue. It was from a woman in New York who had read about my little sports publishing company in little old England and was asking for some feedback on some material she had written.

I read it. Showed it to my wife, also a sports writer, named Vikki Orvice. She liked it too, particularly an anecdote about the writer and her daughter traveling into New York City to see the 2015 World Cup–winning US women's soccer team and the young girl getting to ask a question of some of the team, live on *Good Morning America*. To her mother's pride, and cheers from the audience, she asked whether these amazing women should be getting pay parity with the men.

My bright, brilliant and beloved Vikki died of secondary breast cancer on February 6, 2019, aged fifty-six. A few months later I had an idea to set up a book prize in her memory, in conjunction with the organization Women in Football, of which Vikki was a founder and board member.

I thought of that writer who had sent me a sample of her book and wrote to her, suggesting she submit her idea for the prize and take her chances with a five-strong judging panel. Wisely, she did.

Susie Petruccelli's *Raised A Warrior*, poignant and potent, was a worthy winner of the Vikki Orvice Book Prize and was published in the United Kingdom in May 2020 to remarkable and deserved critical acclaim.

Personally, I was comforted by the certain knowledge that Vikki would have loved this book, its subject matter and its writing. And Vikki was a tough crowd.

I was ridiculously proud to set this wonderful book on its path in life. Now I am now prouder still that it will find a wider audience, especially in Susie's native North America, thanks to Apollo Publishers. Play well.

Ian Ridley
Founder, Floodlit Dreams

ACKNOWLEDGMENTS

So many people contributed to this book and deserve my deepest thanks.

First, I need to thank my family for their love and support: my children, Madi, Luca and Marco; my husband, Armando; my parents Tony and Marion; my siblings Tony, Tom and Katie; their spouses, Gary, Elaine and Michael; their kids, Lily, Lochlann, Darragh, and Brighie; my Cali aunties, uncles, and cousins; my Crowley family; and all the Petruccellis including but not limited to Nancy, Giulio, Teresa, Bobby, Julia, Peter, Sandro, Jojo, Meryl, Bruna, Andrew, Filippa, Alex, Julian, Baby Tapia, Rosamaria and of course the elegant Zia Graziella.

Special thanks to my cousin Mary Osborne for inviting me to the Women's Sports Foundation Annual Salute as her plus-one so many years ago and introducing me to her world of badass athlete activists. Love you, Mary.

Thank you to the neighbors, friends and teammates who helped raise me. Joanne, Romi, Heather, Nicole, Mary, Chris J., Kim D., Tommy R., Timmy, Sara, Reena, Megan, Lindsay, Emily, Devon, Will, Meg, Cobie, Tenser, Chel, Libby, Liner, Bethel, Simmons, Marty, Flynnie, Brooke, Bertie, Uie, Erin, Sharon, Gudie, Carey, Cara, Becky, Jess, Rebe, Bowesie, Ashley, Bags, Burney, Jaime, Brynnie, Nay Nay, Berman, Zotts, Jesse, Tim, Jay, Jodi. All of you who ever passed me the ball, told me "man on," told me it would be OK or got me a bag of ice: thank you. Melissa and Connor, thank you for your friendship and encouragement. Chris and

Mike, the current stewards of the Harvard women's soccer program— we are so blessed to have you. Dani, thank you for all the reading, honesty and love. Michelle C., thank you for enjoying my writing even when it was an email to the principal. Jared and Al, Danielle and Joe, and all of our Manhasset friends who have become family and help me so much with the day-to-day.

Thank you to the amazing writers and editors I leaned on and learned from along the way. Francine LaSala, Adele Jackson Gibson, Rebecca Beyer and Charlotte Atyeo. Special thanks to Rebecca Beyer—you were the missing link at a critical time. You gave this book its shape. You are an incredible collaborator, interviewer and writer. I share this with you completely and cannot thank you enough for all of your help. And Charlotte—I'm so fortunate to have been blessed with your expertise. You are brilliant and I can't thank you enough for your time and skill. It was my sincere pleasure to work with all of you.

Thank you to the fabulous team at Floodlit Dreams Publishing, Ian Ridley and Seth Burkett. This opportunity is truly the most amazing floodlit dream.

Thank you to the incredible organization Women in Football, Ebru Koksal, Anna Kessel, Jane Purdon and everyone. This is the honor of a lifetime. My deepest hope is that I've written something that Vikki would approve of.

Thank you to Melanie McGillick for being such a good friend and insisting that Kely and I meet. And thank you to Kely for seeing me, believing in me, teaching me, taking me out of my comfort zone and out of my own way. Thank you to our Warriors team—Lais Araujo, Justin Noto, Eric Branco, Catherine Bealin, Luis Castro and Robert Brivio.

Thank you to all of the people whose work inspired mine, including Billie Jean King, Julie Foudy, Shek Borkowski, Donna de Varona, Becca Roux, Mary Harvey, Michelle Akers, Kristine Lilly and all the players of the US Women's National Team, Nancy Hogshead-Makar, Andrew Zimbalist, Caitlin Murray, Meg Linehan, Jane Schonberger, Grant Wahl, Jeff Kassouf, Andrew Das, Kelsey Trainor, Amanda Vandervort, Moya

Dodd, Laura Youngson, Maggie Murphy, Edward Ramsden, HRH Prince Ali Bin Al-Hussein of Jordan, J.F. Cecillon, Shimon Cohen, Kelly Lindsay, Majken Gilmarten, Minky Worden, Mara Gubuan, Maryam Majd, OpenStadiums, Sahar Khodayari (Blue Girl), Alyse LaHue, Bex Smith, Suzy Wrack, Alex Scott, Kieran Theivam, Matthew Barrett, Felicia Pennant, Flo Lloyd-Hughes, Alison Bender, Tiffany Weimer, Michael Messner, Jeff Gerson, Alex Scott, Josep Bartomeu, Dale Russakoff, Gail Collins, Ginny Gilder, Shep Messing, Abby Wambach, Glennon Doyle, Gwendolyn Oxenham, Nick Hornby, Deborah L. Brake, Welch Suggs, Kathrine Switzer, The Red Rose Crew, Chris Ernst, David Hirshey, Jere Longman, R. Vivian Acosta, Linda Jean Carpenter, Jean Williams, Jaime Schultz, Sue Lopez, Andrei Markovitz, Jessica Gavora, Karen Blumenthal, Daniel Boyne, Nancy Friedman, Sharra L. Vostral, Betty Freidan, Madeleine Blais. Maya Mendoza-Exstrom, and Rebekah Salwasser.

Thank you to Natalie Portman, Jessica Chastain, Jennifer Garner, Uzo Aduba and Eva Longoria for showing up for the USWNT, and to leaders like Gloria Steinem, Ellen DeGeneres, Oprah Winfrey, Reese Witherspoon, Laura Dern, Geena Davis, Michelle Obama and Melinda Gates for the spotlight in the sky.

Sending a huge thank you to everyone at Apollo Publishers: Alex Merrill, Julia Abramoff, Gregory Henry, Margaret Kaplan and their team. It is an enormous honor to be part of the Apollo family. A very special thank you to Don Rosenfeld for believing in me and my work. Special thanks to Donna Stake and Sabrina McCarthy. Thank you to Ben Karhl and his family. And to the AtaFootball.com team led by Es and Hannah, I'm so grateful to be part of what you're building.

And last, thank you to all little girls who refuse to accept less and boys who refuse to accept less for them.

PRAISE FOR
RAISED A WARRIOR

"Susie's inspirational story, full of hard truths, shows the strength we have within when we harness the power of sport to seek equality and live authentic lives."

   Billie Jean King, winner of thirty-nine Grand Slam tennis tournaments, founder of the Women's Tennis Association and the Women's Sports Foundation

"A powerful account of women in soccer told by the remarkable Susie Petruccelli. A lifelong soccer player, Susie recognizes the life-changing potential of the game we all love. Any young player who reads *Raised A Warrior* will be inspired and there can be no higher accolade than that."

   HRH Prince Ali Bin Al Hussein of Jordan, founder of AFDP Global

"A passionate and thoughtful account of a young woman struggling to discover who she is in a world that is constantly telling her who she should be. This book tells a story about one girl's very personal coming-of-age, but in its theme it is a reflection on the constant internal push and pull that we often have to do, as women, to find ourselves beneath all of our socially ingrained beliefs about who we are supposed to be."

   Kely Nascimento-Deluca, director of
   Warriors of a Beautiful Game

"How we look at gender in sports is changing. *Raised A Warrior* is going to help shape the narrative of the current movement."

Donna de Varona, Olympic Gold medalist,
first president of the Women's Sports Foundation,
chair of 1999 FIFA Women's World Cup,
consultant to the US Senate on Olympic and Title IX issues

"Susie courageously tells her story of being part of a team, the sisterhood of sports, the pull to do more, the passion to help others, and all the growth that happens in between life's most wonderful adventures of marriage and kids. I am so proud of Susie for sharing her story because by her action other people will be encouraged to live out their dream as well."

Julie Foudy, USWNT, 1991 and 1999 World Cup champion,
Olympic Gold and Silver medalist

"*Raised a Warrior* is a compelling reminder that soccer has the ability to change our lives, drive our ambitions and deliver on our dreams. And that it's also messy, complicated and represents far more than just a sport. Susie's voice reflects a chorus of women who have played competitive soccer, and it's a call to players all over the world to share their triumphs and struggles too. There's no one way to be a woman in sport, but there is strength in knowing that others have walked a similar path."

Amanda Vandervort, chief women's football officer at FIFPRO

"Susie's story reveals her highs and lows of growing up as an aspiring soccer player through the US collegiate system. But her account is more than just friendships and frolics. She recognizes the reasons for her experiences, and then those of others female players around the world, when she embarks on a film-making tour. We can all do our part for equal access for girls, whoever we are."

Polly Bancroft, business development specialist, UEFA

"A raw and compelling personal story from an inspirational woman. Susie's journey connects with powerful movements for change in recent history and today. While progress is being made, her story sets the scene for the battles to come."

Matthew Barrett, cofounder of Goal Click

"In my twenty-four years of reading and facilitating book clubs, I have never met a female protagonist quite like this. A fearless warrior, fighting for equality for women, and making Title IX more than just a Roman numeral, Susie tells her story and pays homage to her heroines, Billie Jean King and Julie Foudy."

Donna J. Diamond, book club facilitator,
author of *Book Club: How I Became the Ultimate Hard-Core,*
High-Handed, Card-Carrying Bibliophilist

"The inspirational story of a soccer crusader traveling the world to shed light on how far the women's game has come and how far it still has to go."

David Hirshey, writer-at-large, *Eight by Eight*

"Susie's story is authentic, emotional and thought-provoking. And it couldn't be more relevant."

Rose Lavelle, USWNT, 2019 World Cup champion, 2019 Bronze Ball winner

"A fun page-turner of a book that I think everyone can relate to."

Kristine Lilly, USWNT, 1991 and 1999 World Cup champion, Olympic Gold and Silver medalist

"Just as important as the accomplishments women make in sports on and off the field are the stories about them. There's a lot of catching up to do on the coverage of women's sports, but Susie's journey is a vital and inspiring one. This book celebrates what women have overcome in sports, but perhaps more importantly, shows that whether you're a young girl from Southern California playing collegiate soccer or a World Cup champion, we are all in this together."

Lucy McCalmont, editor-at-large, *Season* zine

"This is an extraordinary book. The author is clear-eyed and unsentimental in telling us of her journey as an athlete and as a person. This is no simple fable of pure-grit-conquers-all; sometimes things break and stay broken, some lemons don't make lemonade. Petruccelli never flinches from that reality, and her openness lets us see our own lives more clearly. You will find no better encapsulation of why equality matters in soccer, the world's universal language, and in life. Read it yourself, give it to your friends, and read it to your daughters and your sons."

Ed Ramsden, director of Lewes Football Club

"An honest deep dive into the timely themes of gender, identity and sports. It's about the often painful process of personal evolution and the rewards of reinventing yourself at any age."

Ethan Zohn, *Survivor Africa* winner,
cofounder Grassroot Soccer, contestant on *Survivor 40*

"A powerful insight into US women's collegiate soccer, and an important memoir."

Professor Jean Williams, sports historian

"In this pulsating love affair with the beautiful game, Susie takes the reader on an intimate journey of self-discovery from a little girl who wants to play at the top to a warrior who recognizes the power of the game to change the world for the better—one empowered woman at a time. An absolute must-read for anyone who aspires to a more equal world/society, on and off the field!"

Misha Sher, vice president, sport and entertainment, MediaCom

"Susie has tapped into an inherent power in speaking out and telling a story to effect change."

Kelsey Trainor, producer, lawyer, and writer

"An extremely moving tale of a young girl's journey through to adulthood in parallel and intertwined with women's soccer. Her political and social awakening (the discovery of the effects of the revolutionary Title IX legislation and its influence on her life, and a shattering of illusions in governing bodies and instead the development of an appreciation for the struggles from the bottom up that have been necessary to force change) is as exciting a journey as her soccer one."

Suzanne Wrack, women's soccer writer, *The Guardian*

"Susie does a spectacular job of weaving her own personal experiences into the story of women's soccer's growth over the same time period, and she does it in a way which resonates deeply with so many of us who had similar experiences playing. Whether you follow the sport or haven't kicked a ball since rec soccer, you can relate to Susie's stories and the wider themes she presents throughout the book."

Jeff Kassouf, founder, The Equalizer